Becoming Waldo

Becoming Waldo

How Being My Dog Would Make Me a Better Human

Jennifer A. Carle

Tate Publishing & Enterprises

Published by Tate Publishing & Enterprises, LLC
127 E. Trade Center Terrace | Mustang, Oklahoma 73064 USA
1.888.361.9473 | www.tatepublishing.com

Tate Publishing is committed to excellence in the publishing industry. The company reflects the philosophy established by the founders, based on Psalm 68:11,
"The Lord gave the word and great was the company of those who published it."

Book design copyright © 2009 by Tate Publishing, LLC. All rights reserved.
Cover design by Tyler Evans
Photos by Emily Tobias
Interior design by Stefanie Rooney

Published in the United States of America

ISBN: 978-1-61566-565-5
1. Biography & Autobiography, Personal Memoirs
2. Pets, Dogs, General
09.12.01

Dedication

This book is dedicated to all of those who have lost a pet in a physical sense and will never forget the companionship.

Acknowledgements

When my beloved, sweet, and at times vicious dog, Winn, had to be put to sleep on August 26, 2007, my heart broke into ten million pieces. We had owned each other for over thirteen years. When I came home and saw Winn's food bowl and toys she never played with, I felt a tremendous void. I had lost my father and my grandfather and did not feel the same intense feeling of pain as I did with Winn's passing.

I did not think I was going to own another dog for a long time. I loved Winn with all my heart, but she had been a lot of work. I needed to rest. I went to pick up Tim from school on March 1, 2008. I missed the turn and found myself at the Maryland SPCA. I got out of the car and walked to the adoption building almost in a daze. I supposed that I had come to adopt a dog, although that decision never reached a conscious level. The first dog I thought I could give a forever home was not a match. She had a lot of issues, and I just couldn't handle a "project." A couple of days later, I went back and, thanks to a brilliant marketing strategy by the SPCA, brought home Waldo, the total opposite of what I had intended to bring home.

I want the executives, staff, and volunteers of the Maryland SPCA to know that without their help and guidance, Waldo and I might never have found each other. Each and every one of you has an incredibly special and important role in the lives of the dogs and cats brought to you. I am particularly thrilled that we have become friends. One relationship is crucial to the well-being of Waldo and me. I would never have come this far in understanding Waldo if it weren't for Allison Nozemack Dietz, who is an animal behavior specialist for the SPCA, which is where I met her, and the owner of Practical Pet Solutions, LLC

Allison is referred to on these pages as Super Trainer Girl (STG). Waldo and I both fell under her spell the first day we met her. Our relationship with Allie is not over by a long shot. I still have a bed made up for her whenever she wants to move in.

Thanks must also go to my editor, Jaime McNutt Bode. We have worked together before, but this was the first time she inferred that she liked my title better than the book. Jaime, thank you for keeping this project fun and realistic.

To all of you who have fostered or adopted a shelter cat or dog, I give my sincerest thanks.

One hundred percent of the proceeds from the sale of this book will go to The Maryland SPCA or other local shelters.

Table of Contents

Introduction	**11**
When in Doubt, Lay Down	**15**
Enjoy the Scenery	**19**
Have Spirit	**23**
Listen to Instinct	**31**
Slouch	**41**
Eat to Live	**45**
Testing	**51**
Boot Camp	**61**
Waldo Photo Section	**71**
Shopping Spree	**77**
Learning the Basics	**81**
This is Getting Easy. I Must Be Doing it Wrong.	**89**
A Puzzle for the Pieces	**95**

Teaching an Old Dog New Tricks   **99**

I Made a Huge Mistake   **103**

On My Own (and Liking It)   **111**

The Reinvention of Waldo   **117**

The Real Reality   **125**

Rev it Up; Calm it Down   **133**

It Takes a Village to Raise a Waldo   **139**

To Be Continued...   **143**

Introduction

When I had to euthanize my beloved dog Winn on August 26, 2007, six weeks shy of her fifteenth birthday, a piece of my heart left me. I knew I did the right thing, and I knew I was going to lose Winn eventually, but the pain of it was unbearable.

I made a shrine for her with pictures of us and her favorite dog "necklace." I could not pick up her ashes for several weeks after they returned from the crematorium. I was not ready for the finality of it all. I had planned to bury some of her ashes under our lilac trees; she loved the shade they provided. We were building an addition, and two of our three lilacs needed to be cut down because they were in the way. With each devastating dig with the Bobcat, my heart broke again and again and again.

The work to our house was a much needed distraction for me. We had to move into a hotel for three weeks after Thanksgiving. I felt guilty but relieved that we did not have to introduce a blind and deaf Winn to the new environment of the Sheraton Hotel.

Each spring my husband, Ken, took our two boys, Alex and Tim, to Florida to visit his parents. People could not imagine why I didn't go too. Were they kidding? Five days of a quiet, clean house? Being able to read a book a day? Who would pass up on a chance to stay behind? I could spray on a tan. Someone asked me what I was going to do while the Carle men were away, and I meant to say, "Go to the beach." Our other dog, Lucky, and I could chill out at our beach house, which is appropriately named "Sanctuary." I shocked myself when I instead replied, "Go get a dog."

I went on the Maryland SPCA's Web site and started researching dogs that were available for adoption. I found a dog that was adorable. She had one ear that stayed up in an attentive position and another ear that flopped by the side of her head. When I went to meet her in person, she was very withdrawn and scared. A volunteer brought the dog out to the play area so we could interact away from the other dogs. She did not come to me or play with the toys that were provided. I felt guilty, but I did not feel ready to have another dog that was a project like Winn had been. I just wanted a regular dog that liked to sleep with its head on the pillow next to me.

I had worked really hard with Winn, and I am so glad I had the opportunity to have her in my life, but I was tired. I wanted, well, the *anti*-Winn. The dog I met that day at the SPCA was going to be a lot of work, and I just didn't feel up to it.

I later found out from the adoption specialist that was helping me that that particular dog was unadoptable and needed to be transferred to a rescue site in order to teach her social skills. The adoption specialist told me to come back to the SPCA as often as I wanted. They got new dogs every day. She mentioned that there was a really sweet German Shepherd mix that had been neutered and was ready to go to a home. I told her that I was terrified of German Shepherds because I was bitten by one when I was younger. I also said that I decided to get a small dog, and I wanted a female. The adoption specialist mentioned there was a female Yorkie that was available. Perfect! I could dress her up and wheel her in a stroller or carry her in my purse.

I hung up and drove to the SPCA to look at the Yorkie. However, as I walked into the doggie showcase, the first dog I saw was the Shepherd mix. I didn't go any further. I knew this *big*, black, *male* dog was mine. It was love at first sight. I took the leash I had in my car from the last adoption attempt and took him to his new home. No questions asked.

We had monogrammed dog beds at the beach, and I wanted to have my new dog's name begin with the letter W. My new dog didn't have a name, although the SPCA had referred to him as "Honey" and then as "Bernard."

The boys and I had batted around the idea of calling our future dog "Whibley" or "Wilson." For a girl's name, we liked "Willow." My new dog was not any of these names. He was relaxed and had terrible posture and a chipped bottom tooth. I immediately knew that he was a "Waldo," which Alex threw out one day as a joke.

Waldo was the perfect addition to our household. While I had to train him to some extent, I have found that I learned a lot from him.

When in Doubt, Lay Down

When I brought Waldo home from the SPCA on March 3, 2008, I knew Lucky, our nine-year-old Portuguese Waterdog, would have his nose out of joint. Lucky got all of the attention after Winn left us. He came with me to football practice; we enjoyed long walks; he ate meals I prepared just for him. Lucky had been the top dog, and I felt extremely fortunate that we had a dog in the house when Winn died. It would have been too quiet if not for the Luckster.

Lucky, who is Mr. Omega, told Waldo the rules of the house. Lucky told Waldo that he could not play with Lucky's toys, go near his food bowl, or lay in the dog bed we purchased for him, even though Lucky had never slept on it.

Lucky barked and carried on for several minutes making sure Waldo understood who was in charge. Waldo listened to Lucky and lay down. Lucky was stunned. He was used to Winn, Ms. Alpha on steroids, growling or chasing him if he voiced any opinion. Winn had set the tone for the house, and it had been her way or no way. Lucky was shocked that Waldo lay down without saying a word. Lucky left the room and turned back around as though he had forgotten to tell Waldo one of the rules. He got close to Waldo's face and began barking some new regulations. Waldo did not move from his position. Lucky left very satisfied. He had a bit of a swagger in his tail and seemed quite proud of himself. Waldo got up and continued his tour of the house.

The SPCA made certain that the adopted pet saw a veterinarian within forty-eight hours of leaving the campus. I took Waldo to Lucky's vet. I mentioned how Lucky had laid down the ground rules and how Waldo did nothing but lie down. Our vet said that Waldo was extremely relaxed in his new environment. Waldo's checkup went well. He was sixteen months old, a Shepherd-Border Collie mix, and a little on the thin side, which was okay because he needed to build up some muscles.

I got to thinking about Waldo's chilled out demeanor. It seemed that Waldo had a pretty good sense of self. I wished I did. It would have been so great to have given up my need for control and just let someone else be in charge. Leading was good, but sometimes following was better and necessary. It gave the other guy a chance to feel important and in control. Plus, it was an opportunity to learn something new.

If I gave up control, I could relax and lay down. Someone else could take over, and I could take a nap—guilt free. Imagine the possibilities. Well, actually, I couldn't; but Waldo could and did. Waldo let Lucky sweat the small stuff. If Lucky was concerned about something, then so be it. Waldo didn't demean Lucky in any way. He let Lucky do his thing. Sometimes Waldo would bark at whatever Lucky was barking at, but Waldo had a raspy bark. He sounded like he could use a cough drop. It was as though Waldo had never barked enough to clear his throat, as though he was a better listener than talker.

I tried to imagine what I would have been like if I did not voice my opinion. I didn't share my opinion about taboo subjects such as politics and religion. Even if it were okay to discuss such things, I was not intelligent enough to sound like I knew what I was talking about. I have blurted out really quirky things like, "Tim, I'm not going to cook you brussels sprouts because they will stink up the house, and besides, they taste terrible." Tim was smarter than that. If he wanted to try a brussels sprout, he'd order some at a restaurant. Who was I to tell him what he liked and disliked? But I did. A lot. With everyone.

If I were quiet for a little bit, I'd learn from someone else's perspective. I would not be perceived as

Enjoy the Scenery

When I brought Waldo home that first day, it became immediately apparent that he liked being in the car. I put him in the backseat with the windows down a few inches, and he instantly stuck his head out. Then he put his front paws over the edge of the open window. It was also obvious that Waldo was a risk-taker and wanted to get the full benefit of the wind in his face whether he fell out of the car or not. I closed the windows a couple of inches so that only his head could stick out.

Waldo really thought his life was great. He didn't like to sit in the backseat. He liked to bounce back and forth from the third-row seats, to the middle, to the front. Not just the front passenger side either. Waldo wanted to drive. He saw absolutely no reason why he couldn't stand in my lap and look at the scenery from a different vantage point. If my vision was blocked, oh well.

If I could relax, I could be a passenger in a car much more often. I preferred driving because I knew I'd get there safely. Actually, I didn't know that, but I knew that I would have put forth my best effort. As a passenger I could look out the window and play those car games I used to play with my grandmother and cousin as my grandfather drove us from Pennsylvania to Ontario, Canada. I could play the alphabet game with license plates or road signs. I could count cows. I could count the cows that were laying down in the field and wonder if it really was going to rain. I could look out my window instead of the windshield.

I could not sit in the window seat of a plane. I needed the aisle. I also preferred business class. I did that because I wanted to get out of my seat quickly if something happened. I also figured that the closer to the pilot I was, the safer the plane was because, let's face it, the pilot didn't want to die in a crash any more than I did. How bad could it possibly have been to walk down the aisle and look at the clouds from someone else's window? I didn't like it when someone walked past me (another reason for business class) because I might get their germs. Everyone knows how germy planes are because of the recycled air. If they stopped to look out my window, I would probably have had an anxiety attack.

Waldo, I was sure, never concerned himself with

wondering if I'd crash the car if he sat on my lap. He knew he could see things from a different angle. He savored a different experience from every window. Waldo seemed to intuitively know that life was not about the destination but the journey. If it was his time to go, then so be it. It was great while it lasted. If I were like Waldo, I could have enjoyed the ride and not worried if the doors were locked or the hotel had our reservation or if I'd forgotten something. I could have thought of the ride as part of the excitement of going somewhere. I could have instinctively and unconditionally "let go and let God." If it was my time to depart from this world, I could feel at peace knowing that I lived every day to its fullest without second guessing things.

Have Spirit

When I took Waldo for his first walk in his new neighborhood, he was a spaz. He wore a harness for our strolls, but I still had a difficult time gaining control. He, at first, ignored all people and dogs. I guess his time in various shelters made him immune to such things. Bunnies he liked. Squirrels were amazing creatures to be chased right up the tree. Birds, leaves, bugs, and branches were all something to go after. Waldo had an incredibly soft mouth. I really couldn't imagine that if he actually caught one of these things he would have hurt it. He was extremely quick. He would bolt after a rabbit, and during our first few walks, I was stunned that I did not dislocate my shoulder.

I had been used to walking two dogs together.

First it was Dixie and Winn, and then it was Winn and Lucky. Because I didn't want Lucky to feel left out, I brought him on a walk with Waldo. Lucky was very social. He was the life of the party, but, as it is with engaging humans, the room got really quiet when he left. Lucky spent our first walk barking a greeting to any and all dogs and humans. Waldo was interested in what Lucky was doing, but he was really sniffing for bunnies or squirrels.

I had absolutely no control during this walk. Lucky tried to run across the street to greet a dog while Waldo darted into someone's yard in pursuit of a leaf. I endured this type of behavior for two miles. I needed to be the walker, not the walked. I made sure I walked them together once a day in hopes of training them. Lucky and Waldo had trained each other instead. Waldo barked and lunged and pulled whenever he saw a person or dog, and Lucky chased squirrels and bunnies. So I was no longer being pulled apart; I was being wrapped up in the leashes like a mummy. I was seriously ticked off. How embarrassing was that? Of course this behavior only happened when another neighbor was around.

The damage had been done. Waldo would lunge, bark, and pull whenever he saw a dog or human *or* whenever he saw a rabbit, squirrel, bird, or leaf. The adoption specialist at the SPCA e-mailed me and wanted to know how Waldo was doing in his new home. I had to gush. I couldn't help it. Waldo was a fabulous dog! I went on about how well trained he was in the house and that he fetched toys in the air and then dropped them at our feet. I was utterly in love with this dog. However, I said that Waldo's pulling on the leash was not only an undesirable behavior but also becoming increasingly painful. Walking him was the only time I felt that I might have made a mistake bringing home a dog as large as Waldo. The adoption specialist told me to go online and research "Gentle Leaders." She said that the Gentle Leader was a very effective (and pain free) tool used to correct a dog's unwanted behavior. I was grateful that the SPCA offered plenty of support for adopters and adoptees. They truly wanted the relationship to succeed.

Waldo was technically a puppy and loved to play and be active. He and I went on three two-mile walks per day through our neighborhood unless it was too hot or there was lightning overhead. When Waldo saw a squirrel, which was almost immediately after our walk began, he pulled on the leash and the Gentle Leader. Because I walked Waldo on the left, his nose turned to the right. He stopped in his tracks. When Waldo was walking normally, the leash was slack. As soon as he took off, his nose moved, and he stopped. Waldo got the hang of the Gentle Leader by the time we went down the block.

I began looking around for squirrels and rabbits in order to prepare myself for the great Waldo chase, but I was able to gain control of the situation. When we saw an animal, I told Waldo to sit. He did. The leash was still slack, and there was no pressure on his nose. When the squirrel ran, I kept Waldo's leash very short but completely slack. I praised Waldo for sitting. When the squirrel was out of sight and I thought it was safe to proceed, I would ask, "Are you ready?" If he got up and pulled, I had him sit again.

The first walk was definitely a challenge. Waldo was incredibly smart and picked things up quickly. He pulled; he sat. He prepared to walk again. Waldo was still chasing after things and still barking at other dogs, but he wasn't pulling me. We were walking together. Progress! What a good dog!

On our second walk of the day, I implemented verbal cues such as, "Don't pull," and "Walk with me," whenever I saw something he might like to chase. He listened. He saw a rabbit and sat down. How brilliant was that? He barked when he saw another dog, and he did pull a bit, but not with the strength of the day before. I told him to sit and added, "Don't bark." The leash pulled and Waldo's head moved to the right. When he relaxed, so did the leash.

On our last walk, which was in the dark, Waldo and I walked together for the entire two miles. He saw things that piqued his curiosity, but he did not lunge. His ears perked up, which gave me the signal to remind him to walk with me. In my opinion, Waldo did not need the Gentle Leader anymore.

Because I was able to let my mind wander a bit during that walk, I remembered back to when I would need to hold my parent's hand to cross the street. I would pull them to hurry up as we got closer to the curb. I wanted to go on the sidewalk so I could walk independently again. Holding Mom or Dad's hand was babyish. Walking by myself was a grown-up thing to do.

I only grabbed my parent's hand voluntarily if I was urging them to hurry up so I could show them something. Then, it seemed, they walked even slower, and I had to pull them to the store window while they told me to be patient and calm down. If I stepped over the line from being adorably enthusiastic to being a whiny, spoiled brat, getting to the thing I wanted to show them could end up being a positive, happy experience that often resulted in the purchase of the toy in the window or punitive. Then my parents would reprimand me loudly and publicly telling me that I wasn't listening or behaving and did not deserve the coveted toy in the window. It seemed I never knew when enough was enough or when pleading my parents to hurry up became whining that they were so slow.

Was that why I very rarely looked at anything anymore as I plunged ahead to my destination? If I had my protective blinders on, was it to prevent me from becoming distracted by something and then disappointed when it didn't turn out the way I wanted? I wasn't sure, but I wanted my outings with my children and my dog to be as positive and happy as possible. I needed to praise how nicely Waldo walked, or in my teenage boys' case, thank them when they opened a door for me.

Because I wanted to keep Waldo's walks as successful as possible, we went out at about the same time every day. We could navigate around the dogs we knew would be walking on the street. Our morning walks yielded far less squirrels than our afternoon walks in the spring. In the afternoons, we would also come across more people. We saw the same people every day if we timed it right. My neighbor was getting out of her car and watched Waldo. I told her that Waldo was my new dog and that he was really friendly. My neighbor looked at Waldo's happy face and enthusiastic gait and commented on what a spirited dog he was.

It was so true. Waldo was spirited. He seemed to live life to the fullest. Unless Waldo was asleep, he always had a smile. He was laid-back and really happy. There was such joy that radiated from him. It really was contagious. I found that I smiled whenever I was with him or thinking about him. When I walked around with a smile on my face or a smile in my voice when I was on the telephone, other people smiled.

If we all smiled and made eye contact with someone else, a stranger even, the smile would have spread. It would have become the norm. Those of us who were smiling would not have been perceived as nuts, just happy—and probably nice too. We would have shed our inhibitions and done what was fun instead of what we thought people expected from us. Imagine if we saw a friend and broke into a sprint to get there sooner. We would have felt joyous and spirited, and our friend would have too. That would not be a bad way to go about life. We would be setting ourselves up for success and finding more things that made us smile and have a skip in our step.

Listen to Instinct

Waldo was beautiful. He had a shiny, black coat and a long tail that curled up like the letter C. His eyes were so clear and trusting. His smile took over his face. When he played, he used his paws like hands. He had a favorite soccer ball, and he and Lucky played tug of war with a fleece braid. Lucky had become so much younger because of Waldo.

Having an older dog was nice. Lucky did not leave our front yard if we let him out. The whole time our addition was being built, Lucky would help supervise and check on the workers in and out of the house. If you called him, he came. My first dog, Winn, was never able to be off the leash for fear her overprotective nature would make her bite or chase someone. When she finally was old and relaxed enough to maybe go off the leash, she was deaf, blind, and confused.

Before I left the SPCA with Waldo, my adoption specialist recommended that I research German Shepherds and Border Collies online so I would better understand his personality. I looked up German Shepherds and was surprised to learn that they are usually great with small children. The information also stated how smart Shepherds are and what an incredible sense of smell they have. I knew that Shepherds were used by the police for sniffing things out. I figured they were super intelligent but remembered my bite from the German Shepherd when I was eleven. I was glad to read that Shepherds were very social and family-oriented.

I knew little about Border Collies. Two of my cousins, my aunt, and a neighbor all had Border mixes, and they were all quite different. I knew that Border Collies were used for herding animals, but that was about all I knew about the breed. I had seen Border Collies on television, and they were the ones that caught the Frisbee in their mouth. From what I read online, Borders never lost their instinct to herd. It could have been as innocuous as nudging someone who was standing apart from the group, or it could have been a nip on the side if someone was running and the rest of the group was walking.

That bit of information was very useful. We knew Waldo was as friendly as could be, but we didn't know why he would try to knock down one of my boys or their friends if they ran. Waldo was herding them. Some Border Collies did not feel comfortable if people they did not know came near their humans. There had been cases of Borders herding a guest away from their owners. A reassuring word from the owner usually ended the behavior, but Borders were nearby just in case.

Some Border Collies would take advantage of an open door or window and run away. That too was their herding instinct. One site I read went as far as to say that Borders could not be trained to not run away. It would have been like teaching them not to breathe. The number one cause of death for Border Collies was being struck by a car. This information was crucial. Waldo ran out the door the first morning we had him. He did not know his new name or where he lived. I ran after him. He only went down the street a bit and was caught by a group of early morning walkers and their dogs. Waldo had a big smile on and was enchanting his new friends.

We had a fenced-in backyard. After the addition was built, we had no grass, so the dogs did their thing in the dirt. Lucky was showing Waldo around, and Waldo curiously took everything in. Waldo was skinny when I brought him home, and there was a four-inch slat missing from part of our fence. He squeezed through it. Waldo had his ID with my cell phone number on it and a microchip in case he got lost. Of course, as soon as I realized Waldo was not in the backyard anymore, I took off after him, forgetting my cell phone. He was nowhere to be seen.

I got in the car and started driving around looking for him. Somebody asked me if I was missing my dog, and when I said that I was, she told me a neighbor was walking him home. When I got to my house, I saw the neighbor who escorted Waldo back and began thanking him profusely. The man said that he had just put Waldo in the backyard. The words were just out of his mouth when Waldo came from nowhere into the front yard where we were standing. Fortunately, he allowed me to grasp him by the collar and bring him inside.

When we got Lucky as a puppy, I watched as he dug up all of the flowers from my backyard. I knew I had to establish boundaries and purchased an Invisible Fence. An Invisible Fence was a pretty amazing invention. An underground wire was placed where you wanted around the outside of the house. I did not want Lucky anywhere near my flower(less) beds in the back, and I did not want him to be able to get near the sidewalk in the front. After the wire was placed, flags were put in the grass where the wire was to give a visual clue to the dog and its owner. The dog was then fitted with a collar that transmitted a signal when the dog got near the underground wire. When the dog was about three feet away from the Invisible Fence, the collar sent off an intermittent beep. For training purposes, the collar was not turned on at first, and the goal was for the dog to turn away as he headed to the flags.

After three or four days of visual training, the collar was turned on, and the dog began to learn to associate the beep with the fence. The command I had used for Lucky and Winn was "Be careful" as soon as the intermittent beep began. The goal was, again, to have the dog turn around before it got to the flag. If the dog did not pay attention to the beeping or the command, he would get shocked. The aim was to keep the dog safe, not to hurt it. The shock felt only a little worse than when a person touched a lamp in stocking feet. You knew something just happened, and it wasn't pleasant. As the dog became better trained, the flags were removed from the grass.

I called Invisible Fence and asked them to repair our fence so I could use it for Waldo. The very next day a technician came to update the wire. Up went the flags, and on went the collar. Waldo was a big, furry dog, and he was very determined. If he got an idea in his head, it didn't leave. Of course, he was a sweetie pie, so I didn't want to cause damage to his psyche while I was preventing him from running away. Nonetheless, the technician determined that the highest setting would work best for Waldo. If Waldo went past the fence, he would feel the shock. For him, the shock would not feel any worse than I described above. If a person or a small dog felt that degree of shock, he would feel a quick sensation of pain, like being stung by a wasp. (Don't try this at home. I know how this feels because I walked through the fence with the collar in my pocket.)

Waldo was tremendously smart, and he quickly learned that he needed to turn around at the flags. He didn't know why. He would turn away at my command to "Be careful" and not get shocked. But one day Waldo did get shocked. He was on the side patio walking toward the gate. He felt betrayed, I was sure. He looked at me in confusion and walked to the kitchen door. After the shock, Waldo would not leave the back patio. This was great at mealtime when we sat outside, but he would not go past the patio to go to the bathroom. If he needed to go out, I had to walk him.

I really felt guilty. I didn't remember feeling guilty when Lucky got shocked all those years ago. I hope I did. Nevertheless, I asked Ken to take over training in the front yard. Waldo had escaped a couple of times, and one time we found him in the next ZIP code. That was terrifying when I had in my head that statistic about the number one cause of death for Border Collies.

Waldo's instinct was to herd in wide, open spaces. My instinct was to try to be in control as much as possible. Waldo was not going to be a sad statistic on my watch. His collar for the Invisible Fence was put on and checked several times to make sure he was still wearing it. It was only taken off at night and during our walks. I trained Waldo with a new gusto. I tried my best to not feel guilty for potentially shocking him, because I knew I could never forgive myself if Waldo escaped and got hurt.

He definitely seemed to be getting the hang of it. Like he had in the backyard, Waldo turned around before he got to the flags. We still needed a little work done for our addition, and for one week, our house was bustling with our job supervisor, subcontractor, and other workers. I introduced Waldo to Floyd, our superintendent, and warned him that Waldo liked to sneak out the front door. I told Floyd that whoever let him out had to catch him...*alive.*

Floyd was a great guy. He became part of our family about three months into our project. It was not unusual for us to speak several times a day about house-related issues. When Floyd called me during that last week of work, I always picked up the phone and said, "Waldo's still alive, right?" Floyd always assured me that Waldo was just fine, and the workers were being really careful because they did not want to stop what they were doing to find Waldo.

We invited Floyd and other family members over for Easter. I took Waldo for his two-mile walk so he would settle down and not jump up on our guests. A moment or two after Waldo and I returned, Floyd came up to the front door with his arms filled with gifts. He tried to prop the door open with his elbow to get into the house, and out went Waldo. I hadn't put his collar back on. Floyd watched Waldo run down the street and said, "Well, I got me a dog to catch now, don't I?"

Floyd took off after Waldo, and I went a different way, thinking that I might have an idea of where Waldo was headed. Floyd and I could meet with Waldo in the middle. We caught Waldo and walked him up the hill to our house. Poor Floyd was huffing and puffing, and I asked if he wanted to sit on the curb to catch his breath. Floyd got a pre-Easter feast workout. Waldo wagged and smiled all the way home.

So Floyd ran after Waldo, but was I the one who should have gone because I didn't put the collar on him? The next day Waldo was wearing his collar, and I forgot to take it off before our walk. I realized this just as Waldo walked though the "danger zone." Waldo was unfazed. He didn't get shocked. I heard the beeping sound, but Waldo felt nothing. I instantly removed the collar and put it in my pocket. When we returned from our walk, I forgot the collar was in my pocket and got shocked. It hurt!

That same day, I drove out to our local Invisible Fence branch and said that I thought Waldo needed something stronger than the collar he was wearing. The owner of the company checked the collar, realized it was in perfect working order, and handed it back to me. "Tighten it," he said. I asked what he meant. He said the collar was too loose on Waldo's neck and Waldo wasn't feeling anything. Well, I had a big *duh* moment right then and there. Fortunately the owner did not charge me to feel like an idiot.

I drove home with the collar and noticed that, yes, the prongs were not even touching Waldo's fur. I tightened the collar and took Waldo out for a training session. He flattened his ears as he got closer to the fence. He could hear the beeping signal clearly and knew what that meant from his experience in the backyard. Waldo quickly retreated back to the house. After that, Waldo did not escape out the front door, but we all continued to be vigilant in making sure the doors were closed at all times.

Waldo's escaping terrified me but was thrilling for him. I would pray that he would be okay when I found him. He just loved to have fun, even if it was at someone else's expense. I was the rule enforcer. The behavioral specialist in me made me always ready to change maladaptive behavior into something positive. Like that old song, I was taught and then trained others to "Accentuate the positive."

I got to thinking. What was my instinct? There was breathing, eating, and staying warm. There were so many things that I did that were learned behaviors. I did not come by them instinctively, but they were second nature to me. I knew to get rest when I was tired and to blow on food that was too hot to eat. I also taught these skills to my children because my instinct was to protect them. Wasn't that the responsibility of all parents?

No matter what the species, parents had always taken care of their young. Just as I had taught my boys to never chase a ball into the street and to make sure they looked both ways before crossing the street. I had learned and tried to teach patience to my family. I knew my boys had a hard time waiting for me to finish doing something or waiting for a vacation to "hurry up and get here." Patience was learned with good manners. We needed to walk, not run, lest risk plowing someone over on the sidewalk. We had to wait and remember to say please and thank you before grabbing something. As a matter of fact, we had to learn not to grab.

Waldo became another child to protect in my mind, and my instinct to protect him and keep him safe, to instill basic manners and patience, clashed with Waldo's instinct to be spontaneous and a free spirit and run away. We had to agree to disagree on this subject. I followed my instinct to protect because I loved my family, and Waldo was a member of it. Like my children had learned and were still in the midst of comprehending being safe, being kind and being patient were not always a priority; instant gratification was. Waldo had to learn to check his impulses and be patient, and I needed to remember to allow him to still be true to himself.

Slouch

When I first saw Waldo in his cage at the SPCA, he was leaning against one of the sides with one of his back legs splayed out to the side. He had his tongue out and was a bit drooly. My heart melted. My other dog, Winn, was a sloucher too. When I first got her she would sit next to me and lean into my leg. Sometimes my foot would find its way under her. She seemed very content as I would scratch her on the chin and behind her ears. Winn was definitely one of a kind. I did not want to replace her, and finding a dog that shared some of her charming quirks would have been holding too many high expectations for the new dog.

Because Waldo had learned the basic commands of obedience while in his previous home, he could have very lovely posture when he sat. He preferred to slouch, and it always made me smile when he did. Waldo was a sloucher when he lay down too. He often engaged in the "relaxed down" command, which was lying on his side. Sometimes, he would lazily lift one leg up so a passerby could rub his tummy. His tongue rested on the floor beside him and created another puddle of drool. In my opinion, a "relaxed down" still counted as "down." I didn't need for him to lay on his stomach with his haunches poised for action. When I gave him the "down" command, it was mostly to make sure he remembered what it meant and to make sure he took a rest.

I loved to slouch. I was taught at a very early age not to put my shoes up on the furniture, but if I took them off, the slouching positions were endless. Who doesn't love to curl up on the sofa under a blanket and read? Coffee tables were made to place a cup of coffee, but I thought feet were meant to go there. What better way to sprawl out.

Alex and Tim were very creative with their relaxing positions. Tim would pull two leather club chairs together and take a nap. Alex would sit on the kitchen table and put his feet in his chair. (I actually didn't love that position too much, but I realized there were far worse things Alex could have done.)

Lucky too was very *avant garde* when it came to lounging. One of my favorite positions was when he put his two front paws on my lap as I sat and then managed to fall asleep as he half sat, half laid on me.

Lucky was a great one for curling up. Sure, he did it on the sofa and bed, but he also favored one of the boy's bean bag chairs. Or Lucky would find something on the floor, like a towel or coat, and used his paws to make a nest and curl up. Who knew dirty laundry could be so comfy?

When I was younger, I would stay with my grandparents for a week at a time. We would eat our meals at the kitchen table. The area was very cozy, and there was only one chair and a bench that went along the length of the table. I would always sit on the left side of the bench since I was left-handed. My grandfather sat in the chair. Nanny would be on the bench on my right. My grandfather, Rod, was a man of few words. He was so fun to be with. Some of our best conversations were held in total silence, sitting in his canoe on the lake while we fished. When Rod did speak, he made observations about the world that were smart and really funny. When dinner was over, we'd all go into different directions. Rod would sit in "his" chair and watch the news, and Nanny and I would do the dishes and then try to engage Rod in a card or board game.

Rod and Nanny were sticklers for good manners. Elbows on the table were absolutely taboo. Belching? Forget it. Even if one slipped out by accident, I'd be sent from the table. Since I couldn't put my elbows on the table, I would put my hands in my lap. I would be engrossed in a conversation (usually about me) and begin to slouch. Nanny was the posture police. You absolutely, positively had to sit up straight, particularly at the table. She would put her fingers on my spine and push them in. Hard. "Sit up straight, dear," she'd admonish. "You don't want to have stooped shoulders when you get old." How did she know? Maybe I did. Rod would just look at her.

So I would sit ramrod straight when I was next to Nanny and arch my back into an unnatural position. Nanny would then tell me that I was sitting up straight but that my rear end was sticking out. Jeez Louise. Was it time to go home yet?

So after a week of being poked and critiqued, I would get picked up by my mother. Nanny's pearls of wisdom resounded in my head as my mother backed the car out of the gravel driveway. I think one of the best parts of the car ride home was that I could slouch, uninterrupted, for two hours and be free from the poking fingers of the posture police.

Eat to Live

When I first brought Waldo home, I was shocked and delighted that he wanted nothing to do with the meal at the dinner table. Lucky cried and moaned and barked to be fed from the table, and Waldo just lay under it. Waldo was more interested in nosing around our feet. Lucky would whine and yip to be given a scrap from our plates. Waldo just didn't seem to know what the commotion was about. Waldo would get up to see if he needed to participate in some activity, and when he did, his big, furry tail would wag in our food. Lucky thought the food from Waldo's tail counted as a meal, so he would go after Waldo, licking his tail. The rest of us would be trying to pluck Waldo hairs out of our food.

When it was mealtime for the dogs, Waldo

would eat some of his food and then race downstairs to see if he had missed anything in the interim. Lucky would be in the kitchen still eating his food, and Waldo would lie on the floor near Lucky until he was finished eating. Waldo would then swoop in and eat the remaining crumbs. Lucky would wander upstairs and eat Waldo's food.

The first time I realized Waldo was becoming comfortable in his new life with us was when I had put a rotisserie chicken on the counter to lose its chill from the refrigerator. I pushed it to the back of the counter near the backsplash in order to prevent Lucky from knocking it onto the floor. I went upstairs to put some clothes in the dryer, and when I came back down, I heard a noise I couldn't identify. When I walked into the kitchen, Waldo was on his hind legs with his front paws on the counter and his nose inside the crevasse of the chicken. He looked so proud! He saw me and shook his nose out of the hollowed out bird, taking a large piece of skin in his teeth. He was beaming and didn't get the look of shame that some dogs get when they know they've done something wrong. He gave a complete look of innocence and seemed to want to show me his wonderful discovery!

After that encounter with the chicken, Lucky quickly figured out that Waldo could very easily reach pushed back food on the counter. Lucky was a master at stealing food and anything else he knew he shouldn't and did anyway. Lucky taught Waldo to reach for the forbidden food. Waldo would then pull it off the counter and onto the floor so they both could eat it. For Waldo, the thrill was pulling the food off the counter, not the actual food. Food seemed so inconsequential to him. He ate it and appeared to like it, but he had other things that sparked his interest. I'd had a weird relationship with food for about twenty years. For me, it wasn't just sustenance; it was control, weakness, the bitter enemy.

Although no one is "cured" of an eating disorder, the disorder can go into remission for several years, as was the case with me. Mentally, though, the damage had been done. If I were asked what I was in the mood for eating or what my favorite kind of food was, I could almost never answer. I would have needed to be about to faint from hunger in order to determine what I wanted to eat. Years later, when someone would ask me what my favorite food or ethnic cuisine was, I still answered the question with "ice cubes." Ice cubes were crunchy, filling, and calorie free. They were also really, really cold and caused brain freeze, which was, in a distorted sort of way, a fun feeling.

If I were like Waldo, I would have enjoyed my meal, kissed the chef, and got on with my day. I wouldn't get guilted in having seconds of everything so my relative wouldn't have his or her feelings hurt by presuming I didn't like the food; but I also would not have only taken a small spoonful of everything on the table and smeared it around on my plate to make it look as though I ate almost all of it. I wouldn't linger nibbling at the leftovers on the table that I wasn't even hungry for. I wouldn't eat a cookie or a piece of candy "just because." I wouldn't justify eating a bag of tortilla chips on the fact that I was going to get my period. I would just not think about it. If I were hungry I'd eat, and when I was full I'd stop. I wouldn't feel guilty or punish myself for overeating or eating the wrong foods. I wouldn't weigh myself wondering if that last piece of chocolate made me "fat."

If I had Waldo's self-confidence, maybe I could allow others in my family to eat some of the food in my private stash without feeling as though I was completely out of control if some of the contents were missing. I'd look at a quart of ice cream that had my name on it; yes, I labeled my ice cream, and not think I was the grossest, most disgusting person who ever lived on this earth because I must have been so out of control with my binge that I couldn't even remember having eaten it. I would be able to open the quart of ice cream, see that there was one teaspoon full left, and thought, *I better get more ice cream the next time I go to the grocery store.* Or I could have thought, *I am so glad other people like this flavor as much as I do.* If I had Waldo's *joie de vivre* about food, and life in general, I would never turn into Psychomom and scream accusingly, *Who's been eating my ice cream? Was it you? Was it your friend? Why would you do such a thing? Can't you see my name was on it? Can't you go out and get your own? Why this flavor?*

There are other flavors in the basement freezer. Were you trying to be mean?

Waldo's outlook on life was one I aspired to have as well. Just live for the moment. No guilt. No regrets. No hidden agenda. No hurt feelings—my own or someone else's. Just be the best I could be.

Testing

One year I decided to no longer give long-winded answers to yes or no questions as my new year's resolution. I lasted thirty minutes. I just had to explain things. I think this stemmed from my insecurity as a child. I must have felt like I was being questioned about the decisions I made and the ideas I had.

Alex and Tim had always been independent thinkers. They came up with their own ideas about how to dress, how to act, and how to live life in general. I was "disclaimer mom." When Alex was two, he started dressing himself. My ideas of clothing choices were quickly dismissed, and he would go rifling through his drawers looking for his favorite top and favorite bottoms. One day, he picked a navy blue turtleneck with fire trucks, hoses, and hydrants and a pair of green and black plaid pants. He was ecstatic! He was ready to face the day in preschool, and he was looking good! He ran through the door of his classroom, and his teacher looked at him and then looked at me. I blurted out, "Alex dressed himself, and he is really proud." I felt the need to explain that if it were up to me, I would never have put two prints together.

I explained a lot. The pacifist in me wanted everyone to be happy, so if someone said or did something that garnered a second look, I felt that it was my job to go into a lengthy monologue about the various reasons for that behavior, whatever it was. The fact of the matter was, no one probably cared. Why was I explaining everything?

I enjoyed the relationship I had with the patients in my husband's medical practice. We spent time with them and got to know quite a few of them fairly well. One day, a patient asked me where the bathroom was. I told her that she needed to go out to the hallway. I thought that since she used a walker, the wheelchair accessible restroom would be more comfortable. She looked me in the eye and told me to "Go to hell." I was taken aback. I thought I had offended her for assuming she needed to use the wheelchair accessible one. I looked at her and said, "Excuse me?" She blinked and seemed to have no realization or recognition of what she had just said. She just repeated her request for directions to the ladies' room and then shuffled down the hall.

I looked at her daughter. I thought she would have said something like, "Mom just had a brain hiccup. Sorry about that." The daughter did not say a word. If that were my mother or grandmother who said that, I would have apologized all over the place. Then I thought more about the patient's and my exchange. Why would the daughter have needed to apologize? She didn't say it. The patient seemed to have no idea of what she said, the cruel reality of dementia.

When I had Winn, I would explain and justify her menacing growl or deep-throated bark. "She's very protective of me," I'd say, or "Excuse my dog, she was more than likely abused and has some trust issues." Winn would lunge on her choke chain barking and growling and gagging until I was able to remove her from the situation.

If Lucky were being obnoxious, I would say, "Sorry about that. We probably didn't train him as well as we could have." Most people would be kind, but I did meet my share of eye rollers. I read their look as if they were saying, "Quit explaining the behavior away and correct it." They were right.

When I adopted Waldo from the SPCA, the adoption specialist informed me that they thought Waldo was part German Shepherd and part Border Collie. Waldo really did seem to enjoy herding people. When he would nip at my nephews running through the house or shove Lucky against the wall, I would say, "Oh, that's the Border Collie in him. He thinks he's helping."

Waldo herded everything. He particularly liked people on bikes and skateboards. He would bark and lunge and try, I guessed, to create a more orderly environment. When the local high school cross country team ran by, Waldo was ready to work. He barked, lunged, and nosed the runners into some sort of formation. The runners were horrified. I explained to them that Waldo was a Border Collie and that he was really very nice, although he didn't seem to be at that particular moment. After a few dirty looks, the runners passed by and peace was restored. I tried to explain to Waldo that *we* were the ones going in the wrong direction. He was not convinced.

The longer I owned Waldo, the more curious I was about his lineage. His coat was so soft and had these swirls that reminded me of the painting "Starry Night." The groomer had thought Waldo might be part Flat-Coated Retriever. He seemed to have the same coat. I shrugged and left and didn't think anymore about it.

I had pictures of Waldo and Lucky on my wall at work. Patients would admire both dogs and ask what breeds they were. Lucky was easy. As a pure-bred Portuguese Waterdog, there was really nothing to consider. When people asked me about Waldo, I would tell them that he was part German Shepherd and part Border Collie. They would make their own suggestions as to what they thought he could be or state that Waldo did have the ears of a Border Collie or the tail of a German Shepherd. It really didn't matter what Waldo was made of. He was a sweet, kind, loyal friend who loved his family.

Every once in a while I thought that maybe I should have Waldo's DNA tested. Wouldn't it have been fun to find out what breed(s) he really was? I researched canine DNA test kits and learned that sixty breeds of dog that the American Kennel Club recognized could be distinguished from the dog's DNA. I'd think about it, and then I'd let it go. He was the best dog ever, so who cared what breed he was? Curiosity did get the best of me, and I ordered a DNA test kit.

Waldo loved having his cheeks swabbed. He would have let me swab him all night long. I sent the swabs away and waited. I not only waited, I worried. What if he wasn't a Border Collie? What if he was just becoming untrained and obnoxious? Waldo seemed to have discovered this new game of only herding Alex. Alex would walk into the room, and Waldo was quick to grab Alex's shirt sleeve or pant leg and pull. Alex thought this was funny for the first one hundred times. Then one day, Waldo didn't yank on Alex's pants; he chewed on Alex's leg. Hard!

By then, Alex had reinforced Waldo's behavior by laughing or running or waving his arms in the air. Even when Waldo bit Alex's leg and Alex leaned over to rub his bite, Waldo was being reinforced. Waldo was super intelligent, so I knew Alex could change

Waldo's behavior with a simple command and training treat.

I had always explained Waldo's behavior—good or bad. If he weren't a Border Collie, what would I say? The Border Collie in him made his actions so explainable. People would get big smiles on their faces and nod knowingly that, yes, those Border Collies sure like to herd.

I began bringing training treats on our walks. I thought I could teach him to walk in a gentlemanly fashion and not pull my arm off whenever a dog, squirrel, bike, or leaf passed. His time with the Gentle Leader had long been forgotten, and I didn't think to use it. Waldo responded immediately. He loved to do as he was told for a small bit of cookie. He was working, which the Border Collie in him dictated he do, but we were working on redirecting his behavior. His mind was engaged, and our walks were more orderly.

The big day came, and the DNA results were sent to me.

I anxiously downloaded the results of Waldo's DNA test. It came on a very fancy certificate. I printed up the certificate and began to read. Waldo was... nothing? He was a lot of pieces of breeds but nothing distinguishable. The test revealed that most of Waldo, and this meant twenty percent, was Norwegian Elkhound. I Googled the breed and was disappointed. Not that there was anything wrong with being a Norwegian Elkhound, it was just that the pictures of the breed looked nothing like Waldo. The Elkhound looked, to me, like a Husky with its big bushy coat and sharp nose. If I squinted really hard, I could see that Waldo's tail was similar to the one in the picture. The fur was way too coarse to be like Waldo's.

The test results continued and determined that Waldo also had Great Pyrenees, Golden Retriever, Poodle, and Shetland Sheepdog in him. I held on to the hope that Waldo truly was part Sheltie. That would certainly have explained his herding behavior. I could not identify the Great Pyrenees part of him. They looked nothing like Waldo. I read the description of their behaviors. Great Pyrenees are loyal, kind, hardworking, and love to chase anything that moves. Now we were getting somewhere. The Golden and the Poodle I could see if I really stretched my imagination. Waldo had a very gentle mouth like a retriever and a long coat with feathers, and he was brilliant like a Poodle.

The rest of Waldo (less than ten percent) showed that Waldo was part Afghan hound and Schnauzer. I didn't see the Schnauzer in him, but I remembered the Afghan my friend had when I was little had fur that was so soft. I wanted to curl up into the dog and take a nap. As I recall, the Afghan probably would have let me.

So the results were in. Waldo was one hundred percent mutt! My big, soft, loveable, loyal, friendly Heinz 57. When people asked me what type of dog Waldo was, I'd have to change my answer from Border Collie/German Shepherd mix to something more creative. Because Waldo was found on the streets of Baltimore City, the breed "Inner City Retriever" came to mind.

Waldo didn't care one way or the other. He was just himself, and for him, that's all that mattered. He didn't need to be explained. He was him. Instead of using my time to justify his behavior, I was better served embracing it and gently correcting the behavior that I thought was undesirable. Now that he wasn't a Border Collie, I could train him and not dismiss his behavior as "that Border Collie thing."

I think the most valuable thing I learned about the D.N.A. testing was not to typecast. Waldo was a Norwegian Elkhound mix. There were no stereotypical behaviors with that breed. They were good, loyal dogs who adapted well to freezing cold temperatures. I had to become open-minded. I had to let Waldo be himself. Furthermore, I needed to let everyone around me be themselves. There was no need to cringe or feel embarrassed because someone did something out of the norm. There was no need to explain anything, particularly when it didn't have anything to do with me personally. I was prepared to rest with the determination that Waldo was a Border Collie mix. I would have probably ended up with an incredibly rude, overpowering dog with no manners and no respect for me. I had to step up to the plate and help Waldo help himself be the best dog he could be.

I had to realize that the daughter of the woman with the brain hiccup in my office was probably going through a lot more stress with her mother than the fact that she inappropriately told me to "go to hell." This woman was, I'm sure, doing things and acting in ways that she had not acted before when her brain was sharper. I was learning to become more compassionate and open-minded. Compartmentalizing people or dogs, their actions or behaviors, into how I thought they should have been was never going to work and would have been certain to leave me consistently disappointed.

Boot Camp

Around the holidays that year, I felt tired and disjointed. I would take naps so I could stay awake for bed. It seemed that all I did was eat and sleep. I put on a couple of pounds and then felt ugly. Waldo was a great nap-mate. He curled up, and off we went together on a furry trip to dreamland.

I so enjoyed his company. It took me by complete surprise when I came out of the winter solstice trance I was in and realized that the dog I thought I had was not really the dog Waldo was. He was rude, insolent, and a real pain to walk. I went onto the SPCA Web site and e-mailed a woman who was an animal behavior specialist. She asked me what I wanted to accomplish, and I told her I wanted him to be polite since the

DNA test confirmed he was not a Border Collie. I told which bits and pieces of breed he was, and I remarked that all of the breeds stated that the dogs were loyal and good companions. Because she taught so many classes at the Maryland SPCA and I wanted her to come to the house, it took a while to schedule her. In the meantime, Waldo was continuously unruly, adding jumping on people to his list of poor behavior.

I ordered another DNA test. In order to keep my controls the same, I went with the same company I had used before. I explained that really it was me and not them. Waldo did not act like any of the breeds he was. The customer service representative gave me a brief science lesson about recessive genes and said it sounded like Waldo got the recessive genes of all the breeds. I told her it was for research for a book, and she sent me the new kit.

Super Trainer Girl came to our house soon after we had reswabbed Waldo's cheeks and sent away the new sample. Waldo raced to the door, jumped up on her, and got in her personal space. STG was whip thin. She had a very open and kind face that was not besieged by the wrinkles of one too many bad dogs. Her eyes were warm and engaging, but I could tell those eyes never missed a trick. She was firm but fair, and I liked her instantly.

"Let's sit at the table," she offered. She asked me what I wanted to get out of our training. I had made a list that included things like Waldo not pulling me on the leash, especially since it was cold and icy, having good manners when company came over, not using Alex as a chew toy, and learning tricks. Waldo had shown us he knew fun things, but we never expounded on it. STG wrote down notes on a pad of paper. I noticed her nails were beautifully manicured. Not a chip of polish or a cuticle out of place. My own hands were rough and calloused, particularly my left index finger from trying to control Waldo. My nails were wrecked. They were torn, shredded, thin, and uneven. I was a manicurist's nightmare. I knew I had picked the right person in STG because of her nails. She obviously commanded a lot of respect from her four legged students.

STG observed Waldo. He was nudging at Lucky's food bowl. At STG's request, I did not feed either dog. She wanted to use dry food for training rewards. She looked at me point blank and told me, "You love him too much." Say what? How could you love too much? Wasn't that like being too nice or too rich? It just wasn't possible. She told me, based on her observations, that Waldo was bored out of his mind and was becoming anxious and aggressive. When he jumped on her when she came through the door, he apparently was not being friendly. He uttered a guttural noise and did not try to kiss her, although he did put his mouth very close to her face.

STG introduced me to the commonly known training technique "Nothing in Life is Free" or NILIF. I was familiar with the concept. If the dog wanted something, he had to earn it. Waldo was literally going to have to earn every single pat or morsel of food. STG reminded me what I knew and had forgotten; Waldo was a working dog. I didn't give him anything to do. He was becoming anxious and depressed and aggressive because he was bored and trying to give himself work. I freely pet him and complimented him. He just had to show up and I'd pour out the accolades. I explained to STG that my last dog was so vicious and mean, it was nice just having a dog that was, well, normal. I petted him all the time because I could. Tim and Alex, and to some extent Ken, did the same thing. We were sitting watching TV, and we had a lapful of dogs. That was just the way it was.

Trainer Girl said that there were going to be new rules effective immediately. I liked her very much. She was so nice and clearly had our best interests in mind so Waldo and our family could enjoy each other for several years. However, I felt overwhelmed and guilty. *How could I, a great lover of all animals, ruin my dog?* I didn't have time for much of a pity party; we had work to do.

We decided to take Waldo for a walk around the block so STG could see how Waldo reacted to my commands and other external stimuli. I put his choke chain on. "What is that?" she inquired. I told her I used a choke chain because he pulled so much. She said that we were going to try a Gentle Leader. I said that Waldo had done very well on that. In fact, I trained him in a day using one last spring. So we put the Gentle Leader and the choke chain on Waldo using two different leashes.

I opened up the front door, and Waldo enthusiastically made his way to the sidewalk, pulling me as he went. "The choke chain doesn't work," STG commented. I asked why not, and she replied that if it worked Waldo wouldn't be pulling. Ah. So off went the leash with the choke chain, and we concentrated on the Gentle Leader. She watched me walk Waldo and listened to the commands I gave him. She asked me for the leash and told me to watch. Every time he pulled, she stood still. Waldo would feel the tension across his nose until he sat down. When he sat, there would be slack in the leash. She began to feed him while they walked. STG pointed out that Waldo would quickly come to recognize good behavior equaled a food reward. He was really hungry. He wanted to perform for food.

It was my turn to walk him. He did do three or four very nice, polite steps next to me where the leash was completely slack. Praise, praise, praise. I used verbal praise as well as petting him and offering him food. He liked STG's food more than mine, so he refused but accepted the pats. When I got the hang of walking Waldo beside me, we looked for other people and dogs. The sidewalks were really icy, so we did a lot of our walking in the road. So did the other dogs and owners. Waldo saw another dog and bucked out of the snout loop of his Gentle

Leader. STG got him immediately under control, by having him sit quietly while she readjusted the loop, and praised him mightily for sitting as another dog walked by. She suggested that I walk with another leash attached to his collar so I would have a secondary way of controlling Waldo if he bucked out of his Gentle Leader.

Back to the house we went. STG had Waldo sit by the front step and wait until I opened the door. He was not able to stand until he had been released from his wait. The first couple of times Waldo stood up as soon as I opened the door. Calmly and quickly, I reminded him to wait. He did and got lots of treats. We had Waldo sit when taking off the Gentle Leader. We had him wait again until he was released.

She wanted to know how we prevented Waldo from getting into people's faces at the door. I explained that we had used a piece of duct tape to show him that we needed him to be behind that line. For us, as we got ready to go to school and work, we'd give Waldo the "behind the line" command, and he would go back to his spot and lay down. STG then informed me that Waldo had no restraints or borders. He had free range of the house at all times, and he was stressed out about it. So she recommended I get Waldo a crate. Waldo would be sent to his crate for quiet time. If the doorbell rang, we would be telling Waldo that he was off duty and to go lay down in his habitat. I didn't have a crate, so we used a dog bed. The command was for Waldo to go to his space, visit in a week's time. That would give Waldo and me plenty of time to practice all that we were learning.

I fed the dogs and got ready for bed. It was only eight o'clock, but it was dark and cold out, and my brain was fried. Suddenly I burst into tears. The lesson and all that STG had told me overwhelmed me so much, I had a meltdown. When I was growing up, my parents had a fairly easy time disciplining me. I was always harder on myself than they would be if I did something wrong. I lay in bed that night with tears streaming down my face as I berated myself for ruining Waldo. I told my husband that I never should have adopted Waldo. He was such an amazing dog when I adopted him, and I had single-handedly made him anxious and aggressive because I didn't stimulate him enough. My husband reminded me what Trainer Girl had said about Waldo being immensely intelligent and how he would easily learn good behavior. Ken also mentioned that STG had commented that most people surrendered their dogs when they became as unruly and anxious as Waldo. She said that to show commitment at this level, when things had gotten really bad, proved that I was able to do the work and was in it for the long haul. I needed to realize that saying no was a good thing for Waldo and for people as well. It seemed that my not giving in to other people's demands and wishes would show that I had strength of conviction and also where the other person (or Waldo) fit into the situation. By setting boundaries, I wouldn't have been mean or inflexible; I would have shown that I had respect and a backbone.

I did very well in environments where I knew what was expected of me. Sometimes when I wasn't mentally stimulated, ridiculous and irrational thoughts would creep into my head. I would then take the thoughts further and create my own freakish fantasy world where, for example, I was only a worthwhile person if I weighed less than one hundred and fifteen pounds. When my mind was active in a productive way, I was able to swallow the haunting thoughts of all my inadequacies and carry forth in a positive way. The least I could do for Waldo was to teach him new skills and reinforce the good behavior that he already knew and help him to feel at peace and content when his mind was able to relax.

Photos

MARYLAND
SPCA
Original artwork by *WALDO*

When I became relaxed and positive, so did Waldo.

If I was like Waldo, I could have enjoyed the ride.

The vet remarked how calm
and relaxed Waldo was.

Waldo's
outlook on
life was one
I aspired to
have as well.
Just live for
the moment.

Setting people and pets up for success was a tremendously useful skill.

Like Waldo, I liked learning and discovering new things.

Waldo didn't doubt me. He loved me.

It seemed that Waldo had a pretty good sense of self. I wished I did.

I didn't have to strive to become Waldo; I already was.

Shopping Spree

I was still really ticked off at myself for what the trainer had said about me loving Waldo too much. I felt incredibly insecure and vulnerable, and really reconsidered if I were the right human for Waldo. I had a list of items to purchase that STG suggested would help Waldo and me. I mentally looked for barbed wire to use as a collar and a thin rope of some sort to wrap around his mouth. I cracked myself up with the mental image I had of Waldo with his medieval torture devises. I would never, ever, in a million years hurt another human or animal unless it was in self-defense.

I instantly felt better and went on to the "job" of shopping. Waldo needed to be entertained, and the words "nothing in life is free" kept resounding in my head. I bought a portable, collapsing crate for Waldo to use as his "quiet time" space. I chose the portable one because Waldo would need to use it whenever he rode in the car. All that fun Waldo seemed to be having looking out the window and barking? It was anxiety. Waldo needed to be kept in a contained, dark area while in the car so he wouldn't feel the need to protect me. *That's what he had been doing?* I thought. *I thought protecting me was biting, growling, and eating people and furniture the way Winn had done.*

I also needed to let Waldo think. He was a brilliant dog who was willing to please and really wanted a job to do. The dried dog food would no longer be available to eat out of the bowl. Waldo would have to work for it. Poor Lucky was going to have to work for his too in order to keep things calm. The solution was a ball with a hole that the dog nosed around on the floor to get the kibble to come out. Later we would refer to it as the "tricky treat ball."

What else would have been good to entertain Waldo? I got real bones that had tasty interiors. That was to satisfy his urge to chew on Alex's leg or anything he shouldn't have. I bought rubber toys that could be filled with peanut butter as another thinking treat.

Super Trainer Girl did not agree that walking Waldo was enough exercise. He needed to jump and play and chase things. I bought a twenty-yard leash so we could play with his favorite soccer ball in the neighborhood common area. It didn't matter that every surface was covered with at least an inch of ice. I was excited to meet the new Waldo! Our play dates needed to wait until the weather got warmer, but in the meantime, there were a lot of different toys that we could play with in the house.

The last order of business was window treatments. Every time Waldo looked out the living room or dining room window, he had an anxiety attack. There was a lot of pent-up aggression with the anxiety, and Lucky was the unwitting recipient of Waldo's body slams. We covered a window in the computer room too.

I was beginning to learn that in order to have things go my way with Waldo, I was going to have to change some of my existing ways. I was going to be giving up light from the windows, time that I would now have to use for installing the crate into the car, and sleep. I needed to wake up earlier in order to spend extra time training Waldo in the morning and giving him jobs like "go into your crate." He loved that responsibility, but he didn't know how to do it at first, so that took my patience and time. I learned that I needed to be more committed than ever to Waldo and not give up on him or myself or be lazy. I had to step away from myself and ignore the inner criticism that was playing on a loop in my brain that said I was a slacker. I needed to have an outlook like Waldo's, which seemed to be that every day, even every hour, was a fresh one. Who cared what had happened before? I had confidence in Waldo; I just needed to feel the confidence that Waldo felt for me.

Learning the Basics

The weather was foul, and while we wished for snow, we only got ice. STG and I agreed to wait a week before she came back. While I desperately wanted STG to come over and take over the training, Waldo and I muddled through with our lessons. Waldo was very responsive to the training treats I began to keep in my pockets. Waldo knew the basics such as: sit, down, wait, and the one I had taught him at the very beginning, which was to crawl across the floor without standing to get a treat. Waldo loved his crate. Through training, he quickly learned that when he needed to get away, it was a safe place for him to rest and regroup in times of stress.

Teaching Waldo to stop eating Alex's leg was hard to do. Waldo needed to be reprimanded as soon as he went toward Alex at any pace faster than a walk. Waldo was told immediately lay down in a time-out. Waldo played dumb. He knew how to lie down, and he knew we knew it. He would sit and look at us like we were giving him the down command for the very first time. I wasn't a fan of repeating a command. Neither was STG. Patience was a necessity and, at times, completely impossible. Waldo could win a staring contest like no one else, and he would have sat all day rather than lay down if he thought he could have outlasted me.

Despite our head-butting moments, Waldo began to change. He had work to do, and he was very good at any job we gave him, whether it was to get food from the tricky treat ball or sit and wait until released. Waldo lost his swagger. Waldo stopped panting. Waldo would lie in one spot and stay there without following me the minute I got up. He would get up and find me if I left the room, but if he could see me he was able to lay still.

Our walks were still a nightmare. Waldo frequently head-butted his way out of the Gentle Leader, and I was left to try to put it back on while controlling him. STG had given us a few tips to make our walks easier. For example, if we saw a dog and human walking toward us, we would turn around and go a different way. I also began talking up a storm to Waldo. I only concentrated on him during our walks. Neighbors would call out my name, but I would remain focused on my dog. Later, they would find out that Waldo and I were in Boot Camp and at work. I wasn't being purposefully rude.

I talked to Waldo like he was my long lost friend. We'd see a squirrel, and I would say, "There's a squirrel. He's looking for food. I know you see that squirrel, and so do I. But we're going to keep on walking nicely together and leave that squirrel alone." Fat chance. Waldo would see the squirrel and be off like a shot. This was inconvenient for many reasons, but mostly, my arm was really sore, and there was still ice on the roads and walkways. Waldo's flights of fancy were a disaster waiting to happen.

Waldo had a checkup at the vet. I put the crate in the car, Waldo in the crate, zipped it up, and off we went. We had a terrific ride! Waldo was obviously enjoying not having to guard the car from every pedestrian, blowing piece of trash, or truck that beeped when it backed up. Our ride was only a mile away, but every foot that was quiet was a milestone for us. I waited at a red light, and out popped Waldo! He had figured out how to unzip his crate door. I was as surprised as he was delighted. Up he bound into the front passenger seat just as the light turned green. Fortunately we only had a half a block to go to reach our destination.

The vet remarked how calm and relaxed Waldo was. I mentioned our Boot Camp regimen and how Waldo was responding to having jobs to do.

He got his shot and we paid and left. As soon as I put Waldo back into the crate, he began to unzip it. With a stern, "No," and a tap at the mesh door, Waldo was rezipped and ready for our ride home. We made it a block or so when Waldo popped out of his crate again. The interesting thing was, Waldo didn't appear to like being out of his crate. He got anxious and upset and barked nonstop. While Waldo was in his crate, he was quiet and had a steady breathing rhythm. We made it home, and both of us, I was sure, breathed a sigh of relief.

I decided to take Waldo for a walk around the neighborhood to spend some of his anxiety. That was a big mistake on my part. Waldo was so keen on every little thing, real or imagined, he pulled and lunged and bucked until I finally had had enough and turned around and brought him home. I was furious with Waldo! I could not stand that dog one more minute! "STG," I yelled to myself, "release me from this horrible, hideous, four legged mistake I made!"

I forced myself to have Waldo do one of the commands that he knew well. "Waldo, go to your crate." He went into his crate, turned around, and lay down. Good. We ended on a good note. Waldo decided to chill out in his crate even though he had been released, so I hopped onto the computer and went to my Facebook page. I wrote for my status that I had the worst training session ever.

I had many friends who either worked for or with the Maryland SPCA. One of them was the woman who trained Winn years ago. She responded that she wanted to know what was going on. I was really glad because I needed the voice of objective reasoning. I wrote that I thought I had made a huge mistake. My friend sensed that I was going to say something less than stellar about the SPCA, so she sent me to a private forum. I wrote that my mistake had nothing to do with the SPCA, STG, or my affiliation as a donor to the SPCA. I wrote that, at that moment, I simply could not stand Waldo. I hated his guts. I didn't write in all capitals, but only etiquette stopped me. I was shouting in my head.

My friend wrote that she thought I had a problem with the SPCA. I wished I could have blamed them for putting Waldo in the first cage. I wanted it to be their fault that Waldo had been sent to them by another rescue organization. My friend wrote back that, yes, I had to watch out for those pesky do-gooders who tried to find homes for animals. I cracked up and typed "ROTFL" so she knew I wasn't about to do something extreme with Waldo.

The next evening, STG came over, and never had I wanted more to hug someone and cower and say, "Please take Waldo," than at the moment she walked through the door. She focused her attention on Waldo, who was sitting on the side of the foyer waiting for STG to come in. "Good boy!" STG enthused. She noticed that in the course of two weeks Waldo was so much calmer and relaxed. We showed her our commands, which impressed her very much, and then we sat at the table.

I noticed that she had a French manicure that time. Her nails were beautiful. Again, I used my thumb to rub the raw and chafed skin on my pointer finger. I begged her to get on Facebook so that she could get a blow by blow of Waldoisms. Like so many other people I had yet to convince, she said she would join eventually. I told her that I could not stand Waldo the night before. I explained the anxiety Waldo had felt when he got out of his crate in the car and how I thought taking him for a walk would help. I looked up at STG and blurted out, "The worst part of this is that I can't yell at Waldo. I have all this anger and frustration related to him, and there is nothing I can do about it. I stay up at night wondering what I'm doing wrong and if Waldo deserves a better home."

STG looked up at me with her warm eyes and a quizzical look, and told me words that I would keep with me forever, "You can." I asked her to repeat herself. She informed me that every dog owner on the face of the planet couldn't stand their dog at one point or another. Then she said, "Tell him." She gave me permission to hate my dog and tell him? No, that wasn't right. Then STG told me, with a broad smile on her face, to tell Waldo how much I hated his guts *in a nice voice.* I wasn't to yell at him, as that wouldn't have accomplished anything, and, in my mind, would have made me look like the neighborhood lunatic. When I walked Waldo and talked to him about squirrels and leaves and other people taking walks, I could have peppered in, "I hate you. You are the biggest mistake I ever made. I should have adopted the Yorkie." Waldo didn't understand my words; he understood my calm tone of voice. The tone that told him we were walking together and were both safe was what was soothing Waldo. That piece of information by itself was worth the fee of the private lesson.

I relaxed. Waldo was a nightmare and bucked out of his Gentle Leader while she watched. She said that some dogs had a harder time adjusting to the Gentle Leader than others. She said she knew of a better container for Waldo: the Halti. We stood under a street light while Waldo sniffed, and STG put her spread fingers across her face. The Halti worked just like the Gentle Leader but had more bands and a connector for the collar for extra security. I instantly got an image in my head of Hannibal Lecter, the title character in Thomas Harris's *Silence of the Lambs*, with his mask. I was worried. Since I found out that I could have told Waldo how much I couldn't stand him, I liked him again. I didn't want people thinking that Waldo was a ferocious beast who ate people with a side of fava beans and chianti. STG cracked up and assured me that it was not as bad as it sounded.

I did not realize how freeing for me that lesson with STG was. I was ecstatic to know that it was okay to truly loathe and despise something that I loved so much. We all got fed up from time to time. We all wanted to throw in the towel and walk away from the stress and the effort it took to do the right thing. I had, at times, found Waldo to be a huge error of judgment on my part. I honestly thought the only reason I had kept him as long as I had was because of my close relationship with the Maryland SPCA. I couldn't admit defeat to them; I had to show my pride and put forth to them that Waldo was so worth the hard work.

To be able to say out loud and clearly but in a nice and calm voice that Waldo was a disaster and a big mistake allowed me to let out my frustrations and disappointments without hurting anyone or anything. It was normal to feel as I did toward Waldo. It was okay to have limitations and to realize that some days were just not going to work out. It was okay to cut myself some slack and just breathe.

This lesson reached out to my family as well. Some nights, I wasn't hungry or in the mood to fix dinner, so I told the kids they were on their own. My one son mentioned that the mom down the street wasn't hungry for dinner, but she still made it for her family. I could only try to explain my lack of desire to cook didn't mean I didn't love my family. I just simply could not get my act together, and that was okay. Someone else was going to have to take care of dinner, and I was going to have to throw my hands up in the air and say, *I'm done for the day.*

This is Getting Easy. I Must Be Doing it Wrong.

I e-mailed Super Trainer Girl periodically with Waldo updates. I had begun to take him swimming for the exercise he so badly needed. Waldo wasn't a big fan of the pool at first. I thought his jump into the frigid bay water when he escaped from the house at the beach was a deal breaker. Slowly, Waldo began to adjust and was a really strong swimmer. He was more mannerly in the car, and when the pool was crowded, Waldo waited his turn like a gentleman and sat nicely. He didn't even mark the walls as he sometimes did when anxious. Wow! The hard work paid off, and we were reaping the benefits of our labor.

Waldo and I were doing much better on his walks, so much so that I got a manicure of my own. Waldo was very happy to please and very relaxed because he was given jobs while we walked. His responsibilities included walking with the leash slack, not barking and/or going after other people and their dogs, and leaving the bunnies and squirrels alone. Fortunately, it was early February, so the neighborhood was rodent-free. The one thing he couldn't get consistently was looking me in the eye on our walks. In the house and away from distractions he could have won a staring contest hands down. Outside, there was just too much to look at.

STG walked with us and told me to set him up for success. When Waldo walked a relaxed gait with his ears naturally back, that was the time to get him to look at me. There was nothing else to distract him, and he was all mine. Waldo, very intermittently, began to look at me. "See?" I said to STG, "there is nothing around, he's relaxed, and still he doesn't look at me." She told me to sniff the air. Okay, I thought she had one too many manicures and the fumes went to her head. I did it, though. I lifted my face up and took a whiff. There was no smell. STG said that there was no smell to *me*, but there were tons of smells for Waldo.

In order to keep the success rate high for Waldo to look at me, I needed to scan the area and see if any potential distractions were around. Waldo smelled the dogs and their humans before I could see them. We had to wait for another opportunity to come for Waldo to succeed at looking at me. I always had training treats in my pocket, and whenever Waldo looked at me immediately after the command, he got rewarded. Sadly, there were too many times when he missed a beat between hearing and obeying or I had to get him to sit and look at me. Those were rewarded with low-key praise and no food.

Super Trainer was done. We had plenty of things to work on, and she was only a phone call or e-mail away. There were so many times that I almost got in touch with her. Every slightest misstep made me doubt myself. One day it was pouring down rain. It rained in sheets, and visibility was next to nothing. My raincoat was really foul weather gear, and all the pockets Velcroed shut. There was no place to put any training treats that I could have easily accessed as an immediate reward.

The rain was teeming down, and the roads filled with puddles. Still, I told Waldo to look at me. He did. He drooled. He waited. I had no treat to give him, just praise and pats. He was fine with that, and I gave him the command again. Again, he complied and drooled. Still, I had no treats. Every single time I asked Waldo to look at me, even with rain going into his eyes, he did. Waldo was not being reinforced with food every time he looked at me, so he continued to follow the command with the hope that one time he would get his training treat. For the sake of staying dry and warm, I was, unknowingly, giving food reinforcements intermittently. He got the treat sometimes but not others. He did the command one hundred percent of the time on that walk because he was trying to figure out when he would get the treat.

That response continued for a couple more walks and then stopped. I could not get him to look at me for anything. He had to sit, and I would need to put my hands on either side of his face as blinders so he would pay attention. The weather was getting milder, and we had more distractions. Kids were riding their bikes, there were some joggers out and about, and there were toddlers who took to the sidewalk at a run and could not stop. Waldo was very concerned about those moving things. He took it upon himself to try to herd everyone back into one tight group. I had not received the results of the new DNA test, so I was hopeful that there was Border Collie in him after all. We walked, and I talked. I told him there was nothing to worry about and for him to just walk with me. I praised him for every step he took by my side and redirected him when he lunged after a moving object. I did not raise my voice. I tried to ignore his lunging behavior as much as I could without being tripped and continued to tell him to walk with me.

After that walk, I remembered to call the DNA company to find out if they had the results of Waldo's cheek swab. The owner took my call. He was really nice and mentioned that he thought it was neat the way I was using the DNA information in a new book. So I thanked him, and we continued our pleasantries, but he didn't tell me what Waldo was. He asked if I was certain I had not already received the results. I was positive. He put me on hold to find Waldo's data. I was doing the Border Collie chant in my head as I waited.

The owner came back and was really excited about the results. He was amazed by the results. Tell me! Waldo was almost a purebred...Norwegian Elkhound. I told the person with whom I was speaking to stop kidding around. He wasn't. He was completely serious about the results and had e-mailed me a copy so I could see for myself. The breeds of dog were given a designation. The number one was a purebred, and it went down to the number five. In Waldo's first test, he was all fours and fives—mutt material. In this test, he was a two for Norwegian Elkhound and fours for Corgi, Afghan, and Shetland Sheepdog. The owner of the DNA company was quite pleased with himself. The new test answered everything, why Waldo had such a beautiful coat (Afghan) and why he herded (Corgi and Sheltie). So Waldo was very keen with his recessive genes. The owner laughed when I again told him he read the test wrong and told me to send him a picture.

I needed control in my life. It was part of having an eating disorder. Part of my need for control involved having extremely high expectations for myself. I was falling back on my old way of thinking that if Waldo was a Border Collie, his maladaptive behavior would not be my fault. I could not change the results of the second D.N.A. test, but I could find a way to work with that knowledge and still have control. Positive reinforcement was the only way Waldo and I would be able to work through our difference.

Setting people and pets up for success was a tremendously useful skill. In Waldo's case, I praised so much when he was doing something right that it made me relax and smile. Waldo was work in progress to be sure, but it was enjoyable because I was always looking for some behavior to reward and for any potential triggers for Waldo's anxiety. I had caught my children "being good" when they were younger. It was so much easier to reward good behavior than to take pleasurable things away from them when they acted inappropriately. Selfishly, I didn't want Alex or Tim to miss out on a sleepover or a play date because they were being rude or insolent. When they acted like that, I didn't want them anywhere around me! When I would come back from my walks with Waldo, Ken asked me how it went, and I began to quickly tick off the good things before getting to the "we need some work" parts. I felt relaxed and became more able to roll with the punches on our walks.

A Puzzle for the Pieces

Waldo continued to do perfectly well on his indoor commands and followed the outdoor commands a little better than sixty percent of the time. I e-mailed STG. "We're stuck," I wrote. She wrote that she would be happy to come back to the house.

Ken and I had the most amazing opportunity. Both of our children were going to be away for the weekend. Except for a book signing in the early afternoon, I had nothing planned. Ken and I decided to take a big step, one we had never even contemplated before. We would board the dogs and go to the beach, just the two of us. I felt guilty for a minute or two. After all, we bought that beach house with the dogs in mind. To go without them seemed wrong. I got over that thought process instantly and began to pack for a romantic night away with my husband. I would be able to wear a nightgown to bed instead of sweats because I would not be woken up at "Waldo o'clock" for a walk. I felt giddy with excitement. I felt more like a schoolgirl than a wife of fifteen years.

When we came back home and "rescued" the dogs from their spa weekend of endless treats, attention, and badly needed baths, I took Waldo for a walk. As it turned out, Waldo needed a break from me too. He was off duty for over forty-eight hours and was recharged. Our walk was beautiful. He walked by my side; he looked at me when I told him to; he acknowledged other dogs with a whine but nothing else. So I did what any other person who was away for the weekend would have done: I gushed on Facebook about how wonderful Waldo was. I made comments of my own about my status. If anyone tried to respond, I got there first. The Waldie man could do no wrong! STG was still not on Facebook, so I e-mailed her that I thought our mini crisis had been averted. Waldo and I both had suffered from "brain drain."

I asked STG to look at her schedule so we could have some spring training. Between both of our jobs, prior commitments, and lives, we weren't able to get together until the end of spring. Waldo and I continued our walks and became better equipped to handle the onslaught of bikes, joggers, Frisbee throwers, and lawn mowers that the warmer weather brought.

Waldo and I would see his dog friends with their owners and get very excited. However, he did not show his enthusiasm by dragging me across the street to meet his friend. He smiled. *He smiled!* My arm was still attached to my shoulder, and it was *the other dogs* that pulled their owner over to see us. If I hadn't thought I'd get tangled up in the leash, I would have sung and danced the "Happy Dance" for the entire neighborhood to witness. Waldo was trained, for that moment. I didn't have a time, even with those trying walks, that I ever felt the need to tell Waldo I hated his guts and wanted a Yorkie. I looked forward to our walks. I trusted Waldo. He knew it too.

We began to be complimented by neighbors about how well mannered Waldo was. We both beamed. As we were going through the community one evening, we crossed a dog and human. I did not know the person, and Waldo did not recognize the dog. I must have tensed up a little and got ready to go into my "good boy" routine. The other dog barked first. Waldo responded. The dog's owner looked down at her dog and said, "Leave it." The dog stopped pulling on the leash and looked her in the eye. Waldo regrouped, and we continued on our walk.

All of a sudden, I *got it!* I got "leave it." I finally understood what STG had told me in the very beginning. Having Waldo leave something alone, whether it was a treat under a shoe or an itch he suddenly needed to scratch as an avoidance tactic, meant for him to stop what he was focusing on and look at me. I figured it out! Waldo didn't respond to "look at me," but he responded to "leave it." His response was to look at me! Waldo was the puzzle piece that I was trying to force into the wrong puzzle. I found out what worked for Waldo and got the correct puzzle for his piece.

I had learned so much in my classes with STG, but, up until that moment, I hadn't really tweaked the information to fit Waldo and his personality. I had the skills for teaching Waldo, and he was becoming a terrific dog. Waldo had taught me that he was very willing and able to learn, but sometimes he needed different cues. I had to find words that he could process on his own. Again, I was reminded that I needed to open myself up to suggestions and ideas. I couldn't train Waldo without the help of STG, but I also needed Waldo's help.

Teaching an Old Dog New Tricks

Super Trainer Girl taught me a lot about how to read Waldo and understand his needs and fears before they happened. I still had a long way to go, but Waldo and I had formed a relationship based on trust and respect. I learned to not look back when Waldo was in the "wait" position. I had asked him to do something, he did it, and that was it. By looking back, I would have insulted Waldo's intelligence by showing him I did not think he could follow a basic command. I also learned that we both had and needed boundaries. It was okay for Waldo to be redirected. He was looking for a task to do. I didn't rest on my laurels, but I did become realistic. My goal of having

Waldo sit on my standup paddle board as I paddled around the canal at the beach was not going to happen for a few summers. Waldo was more comfortable in the water and had allowed me to give him showers again. I had taught him that I would not have ever done anything to hurt him.

In the early spring of that year, Waldo and I owned each other for a little over twelve months. In that short amount of time, I had untrained him, accepted naughty behavior, and retrained him. I was still involved with the Maryland SPCA and was honored to be a sponsor of their biggest fund-raiser of the season. I was offered an opportunity to set up a booth and sell my books. I was thrilled.

I announced my event on Facebook, and my friend who was Winn's trainer told me to get a booth next to her. I e-mailed the coordinator of the event to put the trainer and me together if possible. I kind of felt third-gradeish in my request, but the coordinator was very accommodating. So I went and sold books at booth next to Winn's trainer. We had actually not seen each other since 1994 but shared many wicked laughs on Facebook.

After I set up, she asked me where Waldo was. I wrote about Waldo on my Facebook page almost every day, so all my friends were familiar with our training and other antics. I told her that Waldo was not ready to come with me to a book signing. He would have been tense and agitated with so many dogs and people around. I didn't want to set him up for failure, and I didn't want to use my "mean mom voice" in public. It would have looked bad for me to have worked with the Maryland SPCA on so many different levels and yell at my adopted dog. I told her that we'd see about the following year.

Waldo and I kept in close contact with Super Trainer Girl. I felt more confident knowing she was only an e-mail away. Also, I really liked her and wanted to keep her as a friend. She was nothing but honest with me. She didn't try to put me on a guilt trip for Waldo's unruly behavior, but she did tell me the truth. It was terrible to hear, but the truth often was. STG had been nothing but complimentary and approving in the way I was training Waldo. She offered suggestions, but some we didn't do. She wanted Waldo to relieve himself two times, once at the beginning of our walk and again as we were finishing our walk with only a few more blocks to go. Waldo sniffed and marked too much in STG's opinion. I countered that the walk was Waldo's too, and he should have been allowed to sniff and explore. STG did not give in one bit. The walks were for me, and I happened to be considerate enough to invite Waldo to come along. So Waldo and I compromised. I wouldn't let him mark after seeing another dog or something that made him anxious; but, as long as he didn't pull me, he could sniff as we walked.

Waldo reinforced in me that I needed to learn to listen more. I needed to really pay attention to what was going on and not what I thought was going to happen. That was true for our walks but also how I interacted with others as a whole. Waldo was reinforced and praised for listening. I thought that would be fun for me too. If I were to have a true and literal open mind, I would learn new things and really appreciate spending time with others, and I would appear more receptive as a captive audience. Like Waldo, I liked learning and discovering new things. I loved to fact find and research things; I looked things up on the Internet, and Waldo sniffed. Essentially, though, we were doing the same thing. I let Waldo wander and enjoy his walk and come to new conclusions with each scent; I needed to listen to people as they came up with their own methods and reasons so I could learn something new.

I Made a Huge Mistake

As I put the finishing touches on my manuscript and sent it to my editor, I looked over at Waldo. What a good boy. He just lay there until I was finished. Waldo stood up with me in great anticipation...of what? I was walking into the kitchen, and Waldo followed me, never taking his bright eyes off of me. "Now?" he seemed to have said. *Now what?* I wondered to myself.

It hit me like a ton of bricks. I had written a book about how far Waldo and I had come together, and I was wrong. Waldo didn't get anything out of my writing about him. He would have benefited from my using my writing time to work with him. I had written about how wonderful Super Trainer Girl was at helping me understand how to interact with Waldo, but I wasn't *doing it*.

Waldo was, in my opinion, stagnant. We were great at the lessons we had learned with STG's help, but beyond that, there was a void. Waldo was a working dog. He wanted jobs to do, and I wasn't giving him any. Waldo gave himself jobs. He dug holes in the backyard while I was so-called watching him from the window while I wrote. He had started chewing on his front leg again. That was a behavior we had done away with four months prior. I was negligent.

I sent an e-mail to STG stating that Waldo and I were stuck. I was honest and wrote that I could have found the time to teach Waldo new things, but I didn't have the know-how to break tricks down into small steps. Then I confessed: I didn't have the desire to teach him new things. I explained in my e-mail my concern about Waldo missing out on all the wonderful training opportunities. I asked her if we could meet for a lesson, but I also said I wanted to hire someone to take over the training.

A week or so later, STG came to the house to assess our progress. Waldo and I walked around the neighborhood, and I was able to engage in a conversation with STG. I praised Waldo periodically for being a good walker but mostly continued our conversation. STG asked how Waldo reacted to other dogs, remembering one dog in particular that was about fifteen pounds and solid bark. Waldo and I walked by the dog's house, and Waldo did nothing.

He just continued to walk. STG pulled me aside and told me that watching Waldo's wonderful manners walking by the barker gave her "chills." On her arms, she did, indeed, have goose bumps. STG praised *me!*

When we got back to our house, Super Trainer Girl asked me what I was hoping to accomplish by Waldo being sent away to be trained. I explained that I felt I was holding Waldo back. I remembered so vividly my first training session when STG told me I was too nice to Waldo and that he had the potential to become an unruly brat. Not this time. I was anticipating behavior that had not occurred, and I wanted to make sure it didn't. "I'm thinking agility," I proposed to STG. Waldo was so smart and so ready for challenges; I just knew he'd enjoy going through various obstacles in the backyard. I was candid with STG. She had such warm, blue eyes, I felt like I could have told her my deepest, darkest dog owning concern, and she would not have judged or commented. She told me that she would have been the one to take Waldo and train him. I didn't know she did that sort of thing. I could feel my eyes fill up with tears. Waldo was going to be living with STG, whom he practically worshipped. This was going to be so great for all three of us.

I was vague with my wish list of training goals. I summed it up by telling her to pretend that Waldo was her dog and to correct any inappropriate behavior and I would follow through. STG had to figure out her schedule to see when the "great sleepover" was to begin. Waldo and I continued our routine.

The school year was winding down for both Alex and Tim, and I would stop home to drop off one of the boys from school. Waldo seemed curious about my comings and goings. He had me well trained to come home, go to my closet to change, and take him for a walk. I opened the door, deposited a child, said hi to Waldo and Lucky, and left. Waldo stayed relaxed and content until I would come home for good. Maybe he thought his gift was a boy, and a boy was much better than a walk.

I was trying to coordinate my solo trip to the beach with STG's training schedule. Ideally, it would have been great to have had Waldo stay with her instead of being boarded. I felt odd not bringing Waldo to the beach with me, but I was admittedly tired. I did not want to listen to his barking and carrying on for three hours in the car. I wanted to stop at my former school, Washington College, and visit with one of my professors. I also had things I had wanted to drop off at the Kent County Humane Society, which was only four miles away from the campus.

I started to write a constructive, detailed wish list for STG. Waldo was smart, and he learned quickly. I did not like having to repeat a command or wait for him to follow through. I wanted immediacy when I commanded him to sit or down or stay. He was too trained to have to think about it. The car issue was huge. I was so uncomfortable taking Waldo anywhere because his barking was such a distraction. I thought back to one of our first drives after I brought him home from the Maryland SPCA, the one where I almost ran down a street sign looking back to see why he was barking. I also asked that STG train Waldo so that he came when called when he was off the leash.

The dates were arranged, the bags and crate were packed, and off Waldo went with STG on June 5. That particular day was Alex's fourteenth birthday. We were taking him and three of his friends to Hershey Park for an overnight. I really liked Alex's friends and trusted that they would make smart decisions once in the park, but I was still on active alert since three of the five boys were not my own. I had no time to think about Waldo. Ken and I piled the kids into the car and drove for ninety minutes to "the sweetest place on earth." The weather was cruddy, and some of the rides were closed because of rain, but we managed to entertain ourselves from when we reached the park at four o'clock until it closed six hours later.

Back at the hotel, Ken and I, along with Tim, had an adjoining room with Alex and company. I heard them laughing and carrying on. At ten o'clock, I had cut off their candy and caffeine intake for the night so they would settle down. At ten thirty, I walked into their room and watched as one of the boys tried, in vain, to stash the chocolate he was supposed to not be eating into his mouth and the bedside table drawer. That protest rally lasted until eleven or so, and then all was quiet. At midnight, I called for lights out and sleep. We were going to be in the park as soon as it opened at ten the next morning.

In the quiet of the night, while Ken and Tim snored gently, I thought about Waldo. Was the car ride okay? They didn't crash somewhere, did they? STG only lived five miles from me, but with an anxious dog, the drive could have seemed like an infinite amount of time. I had a fitful sleep with dreams of Waldo coming home and only listening to STG. She would give him a command, and he would listen immediately; I would give the same command, and he would run out of the yard, through the gate I knew I had closed, and never come back. I was glad to hear the giggles and unwrapping of chocolate wrappers in the room next door indicating a new day had begun.

The six of us spent an exhilarating and exhausting eight hours at the park. The weather was dry and overcast, so all of the rides were open. We had certain check-in times at the first aid station, but the boys were free to do as they pleased as long as they stayed together or in groups. Ken and I had a blast. We did our own thing and rode some rides. By six o'clock, we were all ready to sit in the car for ninety minutes.

After the boys were picked up and the car emptied, I decided to take some nighttime cold medicine to guarantee a good night's sleep. I slept past 9:00 a.m., which was unheard of when Waldo was home to wake me at "Waldo o'clock," which was not even light out on some occasions. I got up leisurely and headed downstairs when Ken met me halfway and announced that his sisters and their families would be arriving for a cookout in two hours. Leisure time was over! I ran upstairs, jumped in the shower, dressed, drove to the store, bought cookout food, raced home, and made a roasted corn and black bean salad. The house was gross, so I felt that I had to vacuum at that very moment and clean the toilets. Ken said the house looked great and that we would be out-side anyway, but I knew myself better than that. Our company came as I flushed the disposable cleaning towel away and went downstairs to act as the charm-ing, happy hostess.

As much as I didn't want to admit it, I was tired and burnt out. I felt my kids' stress as they wound down their school year. I was tired of waking up early to walk Waldo and train him. I wanted a break. The first way I overcame my feelings of stress was to admit having them. I felt tremendous guilt and relief when I admitted I needed Waldo to be taught by someone else. STG was so wonderful with Waldo that my guilt had eased quite a bit when she said that she was excited to take him for a couple of weeks. I was still beating myself up for not being able to take care of Waldo's needs on my own. I tried to tune out the thought of being a lazy pet owner.

I had to let him go with STG. It was in Waldo's and my best interest. Feeling defeated in my training was inaccurate. Waldo had come a really long way

On My Own
(and Liking It)

Without a Waldo schedule, I took some time off to do some things I didn't normally do with him around. Ken and I had dinner with good friends one night. The next night I had dinner with a college friend I hadn't seen in over twenty years; but, thanks to Facebook, we pretty much picked up where we had left off. I got a haircut. I would have done those things anyway, but not three nights in a row. I would have felt compelled to stay home and chill with Waldo after working all day. Alex and Tim had their own agenda. I joked that we lived in the last "Pleasantville." I knew the boys were in the neighborhood, somewhere. They knew to come home at 10:00 p.m. I was home all three nights before they were, so in their minds, I hadn't gone anywhere.

I left work early the next day and took that Friday off, and Lucky and I went on an adventure. I was so excited to see my college professor. Washington College was a small school. I was one of about one hundred and eighty students to graduate in the late 1980s. Most of the alumni I had corresponded with through the years agreed that our professors were people we wanted to stay in touch with. I felt certain my professor was looking forward to seeing me as well.

Lucky led the way through the labyrinth of new floor plans, and I heard my professor say, "This must be Lucky." We got the tour of the psychology department, which took over forty-five minutes. The building and the sophistication of the testing tools left me speechless. The old psych building was an army barrack that smelled like some sort of spilled chemical. You could have walked through it, peeking into various closet-sized rooms, and have been done in seven minutes flat. Lucky and I left with big hugs and promises to return soon and headed to the beach.

When we got to the beach, it was still light out, but it was late. I fed Lucky dinner, gave him one last walk, and went to bed. I felt relief that I didn't have to entertain Lucky and run around with him to get rid of that excess energy from the stress of being in the car and visiting new places. Lucky and I woke up twelve hours later and got to work. I had some projects I wanted to complete while I was at the beach.

The weather was overcast and rainy. It was a perfect day for doing odd tasks in and around the house.

None of our townhouse neighbors were in town, so I kept the doors open, and Lucky came in and out as he pleased. I always liked the fact that Lucky always came back when he was called. He had flunked a lot of other basic training lessons, but coming back to his owner was an A-plus. There was a nice breeze blowing through the doors, and I felt fortunate that Lucky was not one to run away. I thought how all the doors would have needed to be closed tight if Waldo had been with us.

I had purchased a floating ramp for the dock for the dogs. There was no way to protect the dogs if they fell or jumped in. When Waldo fell in the spring before, I had to reach down and pull him out. Looking back on that moment, what I did by grabbing Waldo by the collar and pulling him out should have been a disaster. Waldo's silky coat made it very easy for him to slip out of his collar. That day, he didn't, and it more than likely saved his life.

Installing the ramp was not as easy as it looked on the picture. I went to the front office and asked if there was anyone who could install the ramp and look at a couple of other things that needed to be repaired. The women I asked were not a part of our management group, but they were onsite and had helped me in other ways over the years. I knew by asking this group for a couple of minutes of their time would yield better results than putting my request in writing to the other offsite company and waiting (and waiting) until they got to me.

Within the hour, three maintenance men walked around the back and asked if my house was where the work needed to be done. I was about to answer when Lucky gave his "train whistle" greeting. One of the men remembered Lucky and told his helpers that they were, indeed, at the right house. Lucky was good like that. He did make me insane in lots of minute ways, like when he drank water, his face would be wet and dripping, and he would come and sniff me. I was actually not a fan of his sniffing my nether regions at any time. "Eeewww. Lucky, you are *so* gross!" I would state as I flicked his nose away from me. Lucky had always had a reputation for being the "nice one" or the "fun one." Winn had been known as the "mean one," and Waldo was known as "the one that gets out all the time." At that moment, it didn't matter that Lucky had some poor manners.

The workers walked back and forth since there were repairs needed inside and out. Lucky led the way and insisted on playing. The men patted Lucky on the head, but he would drop a tennis ball in the toolbox and bark. What did Lucky care if the ramp got installed or the sliding door got repaired? There were three more people who would throw the ball. Despite Lucky's best efforts, the workers insisted on doing their job.

The men continued walking back and forth using both doors. It was very reassuring to know that if one of the doors was accidently left open, Lucky would have still stayed in the house. The weather was on the cooler side, so Lucky enjoyed walking farther than he normally would have been willing to in the heat. We didn't walk like Waldo and I did. Lucky strolled. He sniffed. He was able to stand in one spot sniffing indefinitely. Waldo and I power walked. We covered two miles in the same amount of time Lucky and I went to the end of the block and back. It was a little unfulfilling to walk Lucky, but there were other jobs around the house that I did that burned calories. If the weather had been warmer and sunnier, or if I had been at the beach with Ken and the boys, the menial tasks would not have been done, but I left the beach five days later knowing that I had accomplished a lot more than I thought.

I was a devoted pet owner. I had such a natural alliance with Waldo that at times I felt we were an extension of each other. I had assumed that he would have been bothered by my going out three nights in one week, because I thought I would have missed Waldo if he was away for a few days. I was being really hard on myself by thinking that only I was able to take Waldo for his last walk of the day or that no one else could get him to obey a command. With Waldo in Super Trainer Girl's capable hands, I was able to change gears and relax. I was able to be worry free for the first time since I brought Waldo home from the SPCA sixteen months ago. Waldo's pace was not necessarily my own, but I made it mine.

The Reinvention of Waldo

Finally the day arrived that Super Trainer Girl was to bring back Waldo from camp. I was so excited. The estimated time of arrival was 4:00 p.m. I came home from work and quickly set out to mow the lawn—a task that had made Waldo extremely stressed in the past. As much as I loved mowing the lawn, I also liked talking to friends. A friend dropped Alex off from a sleepover, and we were catching up on summer plans. We talked for quite a while as the boys found things to do in the backyard. Finally, it was time to get back to work.

I looked at my watch and noticed Waldo would be arriving in fifteen minutes. I started up the lawn mower and jogged up and down the hill of our front yard. I had noticed that when I came back from the beach, I had gained almost five pounds. I was disgusted with myself. I was so busy while away, I justified to myself, I shouldn't have gained an ounce. I figured jogging while mowing would have jump-started the burning of the calories, and for the first time, I didn't care what the neighbors thought of me if they had looked out the window.

I had about five more minutes before the Grand Arrival, so I mowed the backyard too. I finished up, washed my hands, and went out front with the newspaper and waited. It was only a couple minutes after four o'clock, so I sat back in my retro Dr Pepper aluminum chair and caught up on the news. I had brought my cell phone with me in case STG needed to call. I looked to see if I had missed her call while I had been mowing. She had left me a message saying that she was stuck in traffic.

I fooled around and got another message that she was stuck on the highway and would be at my house at five o'clock. I sat back in my chair and contin-ued with the paper. I had figured STG was coming back from a training session with someone else and would have needed to go home to pick up Waldie. At five o'clock, STG drove up, and riding shotgun was Waldo. I did a double take. I had thought for a moment that she put a stuffed animal in the front passenger seat as a decoy. It was Waldo!

Oh, this was so great! I watched in amazement as Waldo sat in the seat of the car until he was released and allowed to stand and proceed out of the car. He was on his leash. He seemed glad to see me, but he also seemed very content with STG. I was thrilled to see both of them. Waldo sniffed and stretched and said hello to Lucky, who had been initially very glad to see Waldo. "He's exhausted," STG explained. "We were stuck in traffic for two hours."

"What? I thought you went to get Waldo," I sputtered.

"Oh no," she explained. She had taken Waldo to visit a friend who lived about forty-five minutes away when there was no traffic. At rush hour, traffic was a nightmare around Washington, D.C. No wonder it had taken them so long!

STG sat in the chair next to me, and we discussed Waldo's progress. She had even written down her assessment of his before and after behavior. She had pages and pages of notes typed in really small print. She suggested we go over a few things before she physically showed me how to work with Waldo. For over an hour, Super Trainer Girl talked about how well Waldo had done in some areas and how in others he was not on the same page at all. She had prioritized my wish list, and riding comfortably in the car was a priority for her. Walking in a gentlemanly way was also a priority. Waldo had come so far since we initially had met STG in the winter, but he still barked and lunged at bicyclists and joggers and dogs who barked first. STG exposed Waldo to a lot of different stimuli in order to teach him the correct way to react to stressors (which was to do nothing).

Super Trainer Girl mentioned many training techniques that made sense. Consistency was the key. She noticed that Waldo needed boundaries. While I had let him sleep on the bed and lay on the club chairs, STG made him sleep on his own bed, on the floor, next to her. She also banished him from the furniture. She established boundaries that Waldo needed. She said that he didn't mind not being on the furniture; in fact, he had seemed relaxed knowing what the rules of her house were. She said that a couple of times she heard him getting off of a piece of furniture when she was about to enter the room, but finding a loophole was not the same as breaking a rule.

Before Waldo went to Camp STG, he and I would often race up the stairs together. He had always won. My mental goal had been to beat him to the top step just once. "Waldo needs to lay down as much as possible both inside and out. So, before you go up the steps or down, make sure you make Waldo sit, lie down, and wait until you get off the flight of stairs." In a flash, my racing dreams were over. "The good news is," STG said with a laugh and a twinkle in her eye, "you will now always win the race."

STG said that she had encouraged Waldo to lay down more and more so he would become more submissive. One of her goals was to have Waldo sit and then lie down before crossing intersections in the neighborhood. I had tried that in the winter, but it was such a disaster waiting endlessly for him to obey in the freezing cold, I got one or two downs out of him outside and quit. Training Waldo outside was not productive for me. Any smell, sound, or sight keyed Waldo up, and there was no bringing him back to me to focus. "Waldo's not the same dog outside as he is inside," STG announced, sounding a little incredulous.

"I know!" I said, adding, "He is totally different! I told you that before, remember?"

She replied that she heard that all the time from owners and that, with the right training technique, the inside dog and the outside dog were the same. Not Waldo. Waldo, it seemed to her, had the shortest attention span she had ever seen in a dog. She wrote in her notes:

> Waldo's attention span is very short, and he gets anxious fairly easily. This is just who he seems to be. For this reason, I would keep his training sessions very short as well to keep him interested... On the long leash he is all over the place. It will take some time before he is ready for off-leash work. It took me two solid weeks of very short long-leash sessions to get him to respond to...me.

I was shocked. Waldo didn't respond to STG? He loved performing for her and making her happy. She was surprised as well and stated that it would take a very long time before Waldo would ever be able to be outside without a leash and listen to my commands. I had a dream the night before Waldo returned that STG had taught Waldo how to do "high fives." Every time he listened to one of her commands, he would raise up his paw and high five her. In my dream, he only did that for her. When Waldo followed the command for me, he high fived STG and ignored my praise.

She assured me that high fiving could have only ever happened in a dream because she didn't encourage that trick. So Waldo didn't listen to Super Trainer Girl outside. That was so interesting to me. She added that it seemed to her that Waldo didn't even like to be outside. He didn't know what to do. She threw him toys and tried to engage him in play, but Waldo didn't play. He went after the toy only a couple of times. Agility training was completely out of the question for a while. "He doesn't want to," STG summed up nicely. She then retracted what she had said very early on and said that Waldo's walks were plenty of exercise.

So here I had been, writing a book about the best dog ever who, I thought, was bored out of his mind as he lay next to me as I typed away on the computer. He wasn't bored. He was relaxed. He got anxious when I got up because he seemed to not know what was expected of him. *Same with me!* I was anxious because I thought I was ruining Waldo by not teaching him tricks. In actuality, I had taught Waldo to relax.

STG made a couple of suggestions for Waldo's

and my outdoor work and then got up to say good-bye to Waldo. I wrote her a check. "I wish I could have kept him longer," STG said as she nuzzled into Waldo's fur that she had washed and trimmed that morning. "Spa dog day," she called it. I said that if we regressed, she would certainly be invited to take him again. STG assured me she was only an e-mail or phone call away. Our relationship hadn't ended simply because Waldo had been returned to me. We hugged, and she thanked *me* for allowing her the opportunity to work with such a great dog. As she walked toward her car, she looked back and said she thought she had even lost a couple of pounds. I yelled back that I knew where they were. Waldo-cise, the best exercise ever.

Mentally, I must have had STG on a pedestal. I must have assumed that there was nothing she could not have done for Waldo. While I raised STG higher and higher, I had put myself further and further down. I doubted myself and my ability to figure out what Waldo wanted and needed from me. If my insecurities hadn't grasped me so tightly, I might have been able to intuit that Waldo's laying beside me in the computer room was contentment, not boredom. He was a fantastic dog who just wanted to be where I was. I wasn't holding him back; in fact, teaching him to do nothing was a very important lesson.

I had assumed that since Waldo was a completely different dog than Winn, I should have exposed him to different opportunities, like agility training and tricks. I was wrong. If I had trusted my intuition better, I would have seen that Waldo was really not a dog that played with toys. He was a dog that did well with boundaries. Something had happened while Waldo was roaming the streets for three weeks before he was found and put in a shelter. It didn't matter that I'd never know what it was like for him living on the streets. What mattered was that I had the skills, the desire, and the ability to give Waldo a new beginning. I didn't need to doubt my ability as much because Waldo didn't doubt me. He loved me. I was beginning to love myself a little more.

Super Trainer Girl had planted the seeds of obedience in Waldo, but I was given the honor of being the one who watched the progress of our hard work. My devotion to this wonderful beast named Waldo was unfailing. There had been times when I wanted to throw up my hands in despair and walk away, and I felt so tremendously guilty for having doubts about keeping Waldo. When STG admitted that there were lessons that she couldn't even teach Waldo, the pressure I put on myself was off. Waldo was his own entity. He was smart and kind and loyal. The fact that he was not a fan of rolling over did not make him a discipline problem; it meant that he had other ways to please me. STG proved that no matter how in depth the human skill was to train, flexibility and an ability to walk away was essential to making all relationships work.

The Real Reality

Mentally, I would have loved to have said that we-all-lived-happily-ever-after as the credits rolled down the screen and STG drove into the sunset. Everything was copacetic for about twenty minutes. I fed both dogs and started getting dinner together for Ken and Alex and myself. Waldo found a bone and started to carry it around with him. Lucky instantly went ballistic. If he had given a warning growl, I hadn't heard it. He and Waldo got into a fight. Ken and I pulled them apart, gave them a time-out and went into the toy basket to get another bone so they wouldn't compete.

We were sitting outside having dinner and commenting how nice it was to have Waldo back, when Waldo, who had heard his name, came over for a pat. Lucky felt instantly threatened and jumped on Waldo. I was pulling Waldo away, and it was my hand that Lucky bit instead of Waldo. I begged Ken to pull Lucky away, and he did. The whole incident only lasted a minute or two, but all of us were stressed. Dinner was officially over.

It never had occurred to me that Lucky would be jealous about Waldo's return. That was dumb. I was so busy getting Waldo reoriented, I hadn't even thought about Lucky. Lucky had been our only dog for two weeks. He got to go on adventures with me and had nonstop attention from all of us. In an instant, that had all changed for Lucky. The rest of the evening was fairly unbearable for Waldo. Waldo couldn't even shift positions on his bed without Lucky trying to start a fight. Lucky was sent downstairs to the "mancave" to watch a movie with Ken and Alex.

After it was dark, I took Waldo for his last walk of the evening. I was excited to see what he had learned with Super Trainer Girl. Our walk started off uneventfully, so I was relaxed and full of praise for Waldo's good manners. As we walked, we saw another dog on a leash. Waldo and I crossed over to the other side of the street and continued walking. Waldo went nuts. He barked. He lunged. He pulled. He didn't listen to any of the commands that had worked in the past to get himself back together. The behavior was completely unprovoked. I was left wondering what was going on.

We got home, and I went upstairs to get ready

for bed. Waldo raced past me, and I realized I had forgotten to ask him to lie down and wait until I got up the stairs. As I went into the bathroom, Waldo jumped onto the bed. I walked into the bedroom and told him, "Off." He wagged his tail. I pulled him off. I went back into the bathroom, and Waldo jumped on the bed again. I told him to get off and pulled him to the floor.

While Waldo had been away, I had bought mats that stayed cool even in warmer weather. We had had a few really warm nights, and both dogs were too hot laying on our bed, so they opted for the cooler floor. I had thought they looked really uncomfortable and found these mats on the Internet. I showed Waldo his mat. There were two, and he had a choice of the one he wanted to lay on. It was a cool evening, so I felt confident that Lucky would stay on the bed all night. Waldo lay on the floor in between the two mats.

Waldo settled down for a little while as I read in bed. Lucky came upstairs and got onto the bed. Then Waldo pounced onto the bed. Waldo was removed and shown where to sleep. Waldo moped until he fell asleep. The next morning, I invited Waldo onto the bed for some cuddle time. He seemed very relaxed. Lucky, it seemed, had gotten over his jealousy and began licking Waldo's eyes and nose. We got up and went for a walk. I was excited to take Waldo out in the early morning. Typically, our morning walks were peaceful. It was early on a Saturday morning, and Waldo and I had the neighborhood to ourselves.

Waldo saw a bunny and chased it. I was shocked. Waldo hadn't done that in almost a year. What was going on? I did an about face with my attitude and instantly became vigilant.

In behavior modification, there is a formula called ABC. The A is for the Antecedent. What are the cues and signs that are given right before the behavior happens? The B stands for the Behavior itself. When the warning signs are ignored, the maladaptive behavior occurs. The C is for the Consequences. After the incorrect behavior is shown, what happens as a result? It could be a time-out or a loss of privileges. By carefully observing, in this case a dog, the owner can give cues during the Antecedent, which prevents the Behavior from occurring. If there is no maladaptive behavior, the Consequence changes from negative to positive reinforcement.

If I had been paying careful attention to Waldo, I would have noticed that he did not just run and lunge after the bunny. He perked up his ears. He carried his tail a little higher. He licked his lips. If I had seen Waldo do any of these Antecedents, I could have given him a warning like "leave it." It would have reminded him to focus back on our walk and get the bunny out of his mind. The Behavior would not have occurred, and the Consequence would have become verbal praise and a pat on the head for being such a good listener. I spent the rest of our walk paying careful attention. There was nothing else that Waldo was interested in at that early hour, but I constantly praised him for being such a good boy on our walk. I had done this before Waldo went to camp, but I guessed I didn't think it was going to be necessary now that he had become reformed.

In the past, I had e-mailed Super Trainer Girl from Waldo's perspective. After a day and a half back home with us, he "wrote":

Dear STG,

Where are you? I thought you were coming right back. You're still not here. The other dog, Lucky, is mean. He tried to bite me when I went over to his bone. I don't know why; it's not like he was using it. I walked into the room where Mom sits all the time, and Lucky tried to eat me again.

Come get me *now.*

Mom took me for a walk while the other dog went down to his "mancave." There were barking dogs everywhere. I barked back. I pulled. I lunged.

Are you here yet?

After we came back, Mom and I went to bed so she could read. I hopped up on the bed, and guess what? She told me to get off. I figured she was kidding. I mean, I always slept on the bed before. I jumped back up and put my head on the pillow. She told me to get off again.

You on her street yet?

We came back to the yard to do some training. I wanted Waldo to come when called outside. I knew this involved many, many steps, so we started at the beginning. I had taken off his Halti and walking leash and attached a long leash to his collar. I had the leash, so if Waldo decided not to listen when I asked him to come to me, I could reel him in. His treat was bits of his canned food that he ate for breakfast. Waldo came very slowly when called the first time. He sat at my feet to get his reward. We practiced this many times. The basic training rule of thumb was to only teach in ten-minute increments. We went for a longer period than that because we were having fun. I called Waldo to me, and he ran over with a huge smile on his face and sat down. I took off the leash to see what he would have done, and he came right to me. Very shortly after that, he lost interest in what we were doing, so we stopped for the morning, and Waldo got the rest of his breakfast in his bowl.

I was so proud of Waldo, and I immediately went to e-mail Super Trainer Girl with our progress. By then, she had read Waldo's e-mail to her and was very disappointed in how quickly he had regressed. She offered to come back to the house that same day to work with him. I asked her to hold off because I was sitting back watching how Waldo handled certain situations on his own without prompts from me.

Every day we worked. A new routine had been established, and Waldo was doing incredibly well. By the third day, Waldo did not need his long leash and came running to me when I called him. A couple of times he misjudged his mark and either crashed into me or skidded past me. He corrected himself for the most part because he knew that he had to sit right at my feet to get his treat.

Waldo and I were in sync again. He needed me, and he needed my rules. The lessons he had learned from STG were extremely important, but that did not mean that my own ways of working with Waldo became obsolete. Once I found my place with Waldo again, our pace was easy, and we fell into our natural rhythm. Waldo had lived with STG for two weeks and had come a long way in a very short amount of time, but he needed me. He floundered without my directions and constant chatting to him. I had my own style with Waldo that Waldo responded to. I was learning to incorporate what STG had taught Waldo and me into my own way of training. I was best for Waldo. I got my confidence back and felt incredibly good that Waldo did commands for me that he didn't do with STG.

Rev it Up; Calm it Down

Super Trainer Girl had written in her assessment of Waldo that he didn't know how to play. She would throw him a ball, and he would watch her pick it up. STG threw the ball a couple more times in vain and then tried a different toy. She used a Chase-It toy. It was a plush squirrel attached to a long line that connected to a long handle. He had watched her dangle the squirrel in front of him and did not react. STG then ran with the Chase-It, and Waldo ran after her. He didn't run to get the toy; he ran to get *her*. As soon as he got to STG, he body slammed her.

That behavior had to be immediately changed. Waldo was showing aggression, not playfulness. So STG ran with the toy again, and when Waldo reached her, she asked him to sit. He did. He ran after her and sat again. Then he showed interest in the Chase-It. He didn't play with it for long, but he had learned the beginning stages of how to play.

Having Waldo get revved up and then made to calm down was also a tremendous learning technique for interacting with other dogs. Waldo put himself on high alert with other dogs. Even with his friends, he would have put his head across their back as a sign of dominance. STG watched Waldo carefully. She praised him for sniffing and bowing as an invitation to play, and as soon as Waldo started to show domination posturing, she had him sit in a time-out. In STG's yard, she invited another dog for a play date with Waldo. She revved them up by running around with them. They played nicely for a while, and then Waldo started to put his head across the other dog's back. That behavior was immediately corrected with a time-out.

When Waldo came back home, I had to run with him in order to get him interested in a toy. He seemed really stressed. He didn't know what to do. When he ran with me to the toy, picked up the toy, and dropped it at my feet, he got tons and tons of praise and treats. When he figured out that we were having fun, Waldo began to relax and smile. Shortly thereafter he got bored, and we stopped.

Waldo was making breakthroughs by leaps and bounds. STG and I could not figure out why he stressed out and looked confused when he went outside. We decided that something must have happened to scare him during his brief stint as a homeless dog living on the streets of Baltimore. Waldo was not homeless for long, so I had great hope that he would learn to play and relax.

Revving up and calming down was a great way for Waldo to relax around the steps of teenager feet. Waldo was becoming more easily redirected if he became anxious. Alex's friends would always greet Waldo and Lucky. Lucky showered his guests with songs and toys. Waldo barked and smiled. Waldo curved into his favorite boys, allowing them to pet him from head to tail. When the boys moved in their tight circle from room to room, Waldo walked with them but did not show any aggressive gesturing. He had learned to obey commands given by the boys, in particular "sit" and "wait," and was able to calm himself down. Like everything else, while Waldo was learning about good social skills, there were better times than others. When Waldo seemed particularly revved up and anxious, he and I removed ourselves from the room the boys were in.

On some occasions, I had mentally written Super Trainer Girl an e-mail telling her to come get Waldo. In some areas he seemed improved, but in others he actually seemed worse. He was as thickheaded as he was willing to learn. Sometimes, he got something in his sight and mind, like a jogger or bicycle, and it would have been extremely difficult to redirect him.

After one particularly wound-up walk, Waldo

came back into the house for some training. Ken and Alex were going to run an errand, and I asked if Waldo and I could tag along. I wanted to work with him on his car passenger manners. I did not want to drive and train. Ken and Alex exchanged looks, and off we went. I was armed with cooked hamburger and a squirt bottle of cold water. When we drove by people, bicycles, motorcycles, dogs being walked, or any other trigger to Waldo's anxiety, he got a food reward and verbal praise for ignoring the stimulus. If Waldo perked up his ears and looked curious about the stressor, STG had told me to give him the warning command, which was, "Leave it." If Waldo listened and relaxed and ignored it, he got a *ton* of verbal praise. If Waldo did not listen to "Leave it" and began to bark, he was reprimanded with a disappointed sounding "No" and a squirt from the water bottle.

We drove on the highway at first. Ken wanted to set Waldo up for success by keeping the drive short and as stimuli free as possible. A motorcycle rode by us, and Waldo perked up his ears. I didn't get the chance to say anything to him because the motorcycle had caught me unaware and had passed us. Waldo did nothing. He got a food treat and lots of verbal praise. Ken and Alex were stunned! Alex reached back and told Waldo what a good boy he was.

When we reached the destination, Waldo had to sit quietly in the car. We were in a busy parking lot, and he saw people. He did nothing! Big praise and treats! I asked Ken if we could take the longer route home and bypass the highway. Because Ken still wanted Waldo to succeed, he asked me if I was sure. I said I was, and off we went. We drove past people waiting for the bus. Nothing. Big treats. We saw two motorcyclists at the intersection across from us. They weren't revving their engines, but the riders each had on skull masks. All four of us looked at them. Waldo did nothing! He was not fazed by anything on the sidewalks and streets around him. I did not need the squirt bottle at all, but I did need to replenish my treats.

Waldo calmed himself down.

I needed to get back to basics in my thinking and my attitude, and Waldo taught me that. There were areas of Waldo's training that were minimally, if at all, improved. I could have focused solely on those things, but Waldo and I would have become frustrated. I was learning to compartmentalize my goals for Waldo and myself. By switching gears by seeing what else Waldo could do, I had wiped the slate clean and became open-minded.

Waldo was anxious to please. He loved to hear what a good boy he was and to get treats. He found ways to relax, and I became more relaxed too. I was able to spot potential stressors to Waldo and redirect him in a calm and positive way. I was no longer tensing up in anticipation of what Waldo's reaction might be to certain stimuli. Waldo and I fed off of each other's stress. I was reminded of something I already knew, which was Waldo could feel my anxiety. When I became relaxed and positive, so did Waldo.

It Takes a Village to Raise a Waldo

I had a fan page set up on Facebook. It was designed primarily to promote my books, but I also used it to let people know what was going on in the community that was related to animal rescue shelters and talks I was giving. The Maryland SPCA held social events throughout the summer months that they called "Wine and Wag." I mentioned the date and time of the first event on my fan page and encouraged people to come to meet Waldo. The event was going to be an enormous step in training. Wine and Wag involved being in a car, interacting with other dogs, and manipulating around booths. I e-mailed Super Trainer Girl and asked if she would be at the event and if she had any advice for me. She told me what I had already planned to do: walk and train him first to tire him out and get there early.

I e-mailed a couple other people that I knew would have offered help if at the event, and they were not attending. I got my squirt bottle and treats, and Ken drove us to Wine and Wag. We got there as soon as the event began, and it was mobbed with people and dogs. Apparently getting to the event early was a strategy used by most pet owners. I walked Waldo around the periphery, and he immediately began marking his territory. He was anxious and uncomfortable. I introduced Ken to my SPCA friends and told everyone that this was part of Waldo's training. People began to remark what a good boy Waldo was and how great he was doing.

I introduced Ken to the executive director of the SPCA. She and I had become friendly over the course of that year, and I knew not to have performance anxiety. But, still, she was the director, and I really did not want Waldo to choose that time to bark and lunge and carry on. I told the director that STG was working with Waldo and me and that he had just come back from living with her the week before. The director said something to me that I did not expect. She thanked me for working with Waldo instead of returning him to the SPCA as "damaged goods."

Because we did have an easy rapport, I told her that once I found out I could tell Waldo in my "good dog voice" how much I hated him, the pressure was off. I had confessed and felt much better for it. As we spoke, Waldo got uppity around another dog. He did not "leave it," and I was forced to squirt him with my water bottle. The director commented on Waldo's dominating stance. We continued to speak, and again, Waldo demonstrated dominating behavior around another dog. I told Waldo to "Leave it" and reached for the water bottle. "Good boy," the director commented to Waldo. I had my bottle in hand and was ready, and the director subtly shook her head and said, "He listened to you." I was elated! Waldo was sitting very politely and patiently, and the director praised him. She helped me help Waldo.

As we parted ways, she told me where the campus could get crowded and where to walk a quieter, less distracting path. The food looked amazing. I knew I was forever away from being able to amble up to the food tent with Waldo, take a plate, and eat and walk him at the same time. There was one little test I wanted to try. Ken was up with the food and beverages, and I asked if he could get me a diet soda. Ken knew what I wanted to try and asked if I wanted water instead. I was sure I wanted the soda. Ken handed it me, and I opened it. I took a sip. Waldo just stood there looking around. We did it! We achieved a huge step in a goal of mine, which was to be able to walk him and drink a cup of coffee. I took another sip and praised Waldo as he stood nicely next to me. I got up the nerve to walk with him. My can of soda was still full, but there was a little leeway if Waldo acted up. I

To Be Continued...

When I thought back to the beginning of my adventure with Waldo, I realized something that surprised me, although it really shouldn't have. I didn't have to strive to become Waldo; I already was. Waldo was clearly neurotic and anxious, just like me. Super Trainer Girl told me that I didn't make Waldo anxious; he was anxious on his own. I had assumed my anxiety and neurosis had rubbed off on Waldo, just as I had thought my anxiety might have spread to Winn way back then. The whole thought of causing my dog anxiety made me stressed.

Waldo was an absolutely beautiful dog. He drew people in with his big eyes and his asymmetrical ears and that amazing tail. He loved to be patted and talked to, particularly by calm adults and children. He was a lovely addition to our home. Waldo handled himself as well as he could in social situations, but if he lingered too long, he would become anxious. I was like that too. In social situations, I tended to draw people to me. I always had a funny story about something, and I was very entertaining. I had an odd take on the world and openly made observations about my perceptions. The reality of it was that it was really hard to be me.

A friend, who is also an author, asked me how I dealt with book signings. I told her the truth, which was that I absolutely loved them. Customers had their story to share, and it was an honor to hear them; after all, I had shared with them. My friend said she liked them when she was younger and writing in a different genre. In the present day, she found herself with a case of stage fright. I told her that the whole idea of being in the spotlight and "on" made me really wound up. I felt I needed to give people a show of some sort. I also confessed that in real life I hated being in the spotlight and tried to live my life under the radar. After my book signings, I would gather up my things, speak with and thank the book-sellers, load up my car, and attempt to put the key in the ignition with a very shaky and jittery hand. I held my hands out in front of me and was amazed that I could have kept the pen still enough to sign books; being "on cue" made me do that. I tended to take a nap after the signings. I needed to unwind.

Waldo handled himself well in certain situations.

When it was his time to move along, however, I needed to understand that and remove him from the stressor. Waldo and I had a deep bond. We trusted each other. He did many things that would have been considered "normal" for other dogs but were excruciating stressors for him. He wanted to please me, but he also let me know when he was uncomfortable by licking his lips. Waldo licked his lips and then panted as his anxiety level increased. If I did not remove him from the situation, he would act in an inappropriate way. The more stressed he was, the more seemingly innocuous thing would set him off until we were a tangled mess of a pulled leash, cockeyed Halti, and sweat. Waldo would have to take a nap in order to recover.

There were certain situations in my life that I tried to avoid. I was not a fan of elevators, so I tried to take the steps as often as possible. I told other people I was being heart smart, but the truth was, I didn't want to get stuck and use up all the air and suffocate. I was conscious of germs. While I didn't walk around people wearing a mask, I had bottles of antibacterial wash and wet hand wipes in my purse. No shopping cart went unwiped. I used two: one for my hands and one for the cart. I never used the same one for both tasks for fear of recycling the germs onto myself. I knew that about me. I didn't hurt anyone when I poured a huge smear of antibacterial wash on my hands. That was me.

Waldo also had his quirks and anxieties that made him who he was. I exposed him to new situations, but I needed to know when he had reached his saturation level. On that point, Waldo and I had much more work to do. In the eight days I had him back after his stint with Super Trainer Girl, he was better in many ways and little to no better in others. I was learning to read his body language in order to judge when he had enough of his environment. We both were a work in progress. I could not touch a grocery cart without sanitizing it first, and Waldo could not stand bicycles. Was he ever going to cheer on the bike competitors at the Tour de France? No way, but I hoped to get him to the point that he would be able to leave a family riding their bikes through the neighborhood alone. I didn't want Waldo to stop being neurotic. I didn't think that was possible. I certainly hadn't stopped my neurosis; I just figured out a way to work it into my life. Part of my charm is, indeed, my neurosis. Waldo was very charming and engaging as well. We were both doing the best we could and were striving to incorporate coping skills.

I looked forward to working with Waldo. I knew there would be awful days. They didn't happen very often, but they did happen. I also knew that on some days I would run out of training treats because Waldo handled himself so well with stressors. I was excited to have the opportunity to be in Waldo's life. He was a truly wonderful dog. I felt relief knowing that Super Trainer Girl was only an e-mail or phone call away. I also felt relief that I was capable of asking for help with Waldo and realizing that it was going to take many people to help me help Waldo.